RUSSIAN ROOT LIST

With a Sketch of Word Formation

Charles E. Gribble

Second Edition

Slavica Publishers, Inc.
Columbus, Ohio

Slavica publishes a wide variety of scholarly books and textbooks on the languages, peoples, literatures, cultures, history, etc. of the USSR and Eastern Europe. For a complete catalog of books and journals from Slavica, with prices and ordering information, write to:

Slavica Publishers, Inc.
PO Box 14388
Columbus, Ohio 43214

ISBN: 0-89357-052-4.

Text set by Patricia Hansen.

All statements of fact and opinion are those of the author, and may or may not agree with those of the publisher, which takes no responsibility for them.

Printed in the United States of America.

Посвящается

Дорогому Учителю

и Другу,

Профессору

Московского Университета

Владимиру Андреевичу Звегинцеву

CONTENTS

"Смотри в корень!"

-- Козьма Прутков

INTRODUCTION

No matter which textbook or method a student uses in learning Russian, he or she eventually begins to realize that most Russian words can be divided into smaller elements, and that in turn, one can often guess the meaning of new words by knowing the meaning of their component parts. The accuracy of this idea is confirmed by Russians themselves, who sometimes make up new words, either deliberately or inadvertently. Mayakovsky is famous for his neologisms. On a less literary (and less literate) level, amusing neologisms are often cited in Крокодил, the Soviet humor magazine: „Коллектив бани в августе месяце борется за 16 тысяч человекопомывок" "The staff of the bathhouse is striving for 16 thousand man-washings in the month of August" (sign on a public bath in Novokuznetsk), or „Твистунов на мороз!" "Out into the cold with twist-dancers!" (sign in a village clubhouse).

As soon as a student learns to analyze Russian words, he has acquired a powerful tool to help him understand and remember the tens of thousands of words that he will need to know in order to control spoken and written Russian. Unfortunately, many textbooks pay little or no attention to word formation and vocabulary development. The student and teacher will find in this booklet the materials necessary for building vocabulary rapidly and efficiently. It will not eliminate the need for memorization, but it will greatly diminish the amount required.

Russian Root List (RRL) is not intended to be a full exposition of Russian word formation, which would require a book many times larger than this one. *RRL* is intended for use either with a teacher or with a serious book on Russian word formation, such as Charles Townsend's *Russian Word-Formation* (originally published by McGraw-Hill, New York, 1968; available since 1975 in a corrected reprint from Slavica Publishers, Columbus, Ohio). See the *Bibliography* in this book for more works on the subject of Russian word formation. Most students will find, however, that once they have mastered the principles of Russian word formation, it will be easy to continue building vocabulary with this booklet alone. Since it is not intended to replace a teacher or a more complete reference book, the lists of prefixes and suffixes are not exhaustive, and such topics as conjugation and declension are not treated at all. The information in *RRL* will suffice for most reading, but the student must not hestitate to refer questions to a teacher or to consult Townsend or one of the other books mentioned in the *Bibliography*.

This list is designed for students at all levels, and I have accordingly included much material which might seem overly obvious to some people. Teaching experience shows that what is obvious to some is not so obvious to many beginners. No book can possibly include all information and anticipate all questions, especially if it is to keep within reasonable limits of size and price. My judgement of what to put in and what to leave out is based largely upon over twenty years of teaching Russian and upon the suggestions of my friends and students who have used previous versions of the list. When I began compiling the first version nearly twenty years ago, in response to a suggestion by Alexander Lipson, I assumed that the whole job would be relatively quick and easy. It has turned out to be just the opposite. The list was used at various schools for ten years and was revised and expanded four times before it was printed in the First Edition of 1973. Relatively few comments were received in response to the First Edition, but they have been taken into account in preparing this revision. In spite of all the revisions, I am still uncertain about the best treatment of a number of problems.

The primary orientation of this booklet is pedagogical, and the choice and exposition of material have been dictated almost exclusively by pedagogical considerations. If I seem to be guilty of omitting material, oversimplification, or unjustified (from a historical point of view) separation or connection of roots, then I ask the reader to remember that this booklet is not intended to be a scholarly treatise (although I hope that considerable scholarship has gone into its preparation). A student would not start learning Russian by sitting down with the Academy Grammar and the 17-volume Academy Dictionary;

neither should he or she be obliged to learn all the
intricate details that happen to delight me and other
linguists. I hope that many students will move on
from this booklet to more advanced work, but as the
proverb says, „Лиха беда начало", and I don't want to
complicate the beginning any more than necessary.

The following section, *How to Use This Book*,
contains information on the structure of Russian
roots, the changes they undergo, and how they are
combined with prefixes and suffixes to make words.
Tables of the basic meanings of prefixes and suffixes
precede a selected bibliography, which concludes the
preliminary material.

NOTE TO THE SECOND EDITION

It had been my original intention to make a
thorough revision for the Second Edition. However,
very few comments have been received, and the time
pressures of running Slavica in addition to being a
full-time college professor have simply been too much.
This book has been out of print for nearly three
years now, and rather than take more time in the hope
of getting time to do the planned major revision, I
have decided to get the book out again in a retyped
version with some minor changes and corrections. The
section which most needs updating is the *Bibliography*.
I have made some changes and additions, but would
have preferred to have the time to make major additions. Suggestions and corrections for a new edition
will still be most welcome.

ACKNOWLEDGEMENTS

Many of my friends, colleagues, and students have
made suggestions and corrections to each of the five
versions of the root list, and it is a pleasure to
thank them here. Like most beginning Russian teachers
who were in Cambridge, Mass. in the late 1950's and
early 1960's, I owe a great debt to Alexander Lipson,
whose brilliant teaching first showed me how many
theoretical concepts could be applied directly in the
teaching of Russian. During the following years he
continued to be a source of advice and inspiration.
I hope that this booklet provides some justification
for the time and encouragement which he gave me so
generously. Alex's untimely death in 1980 has pre-
vented him from seeing this new edition, but many
books besides this one now bear testimony to the
influence of his genius. I miss his friendship even
more than I miss his intellectual stimulation.

Useful ideas and concepts have also come from

Professor Horace G. Lunt's (unpublished) second-year Russian materials, with which I taught in the late 1950's and early 1960's. Special thanks go to Charles Townsend and Hugh Olmsted, with whom I had a continuing discussion of Russian roots and how to present them in teaching, and to Catherine Chvany, who has twice given me a detailed set of suggestions. Wayles Browne provided the only detailed comments on the First Edition after publication. Valuable suggestions on earlier versions came from Ruth Golush, David Hanson, Ariadna Ivanovna Kuznecova, Maurice Levin, Lawrence Newman, Jan Perkowski, Robert Rothstein, Ernest Scatton, Michael Shapiro, Dorothy Soudakoff, Stephen Soudakoff, and Robert Szulkin. I am very grateful to all of them. The blame for mistakes and omissions must really be mine alone, since I have in some cases adopted a solution or method of presentation against the advice of others. Criticism and suggestions for the next edition of this book will be most welcome and can be sent to me in care of the publisher.

I would like to thank Clayton Dawson, Ariadna Ivanovna Kuznecova, and Stephen Marder for their reviews of the First Edition. A reviewer in *SEER* found nothing new in the book, which, in my opinion, says more about his perceptiveness or lack of it than it says about the book.

Patricia Hansen has typed this edition in her usual expert way and caught some mistakes in the process; I am deeply grateful to her.

This work is dedicated with great respect and even more affection to my teacher and friend, Professor Vladimir Andreevič Zvegincev of Moscow State University. It is my hope that by making the study of Russian easier and more efficient, this booklet will contribute to ever increasing mutual understanding and friendship between our peoples.

October, 1981
Columbus, Ohio   Charles E. Gribble

HOW TO USE THIS BOOK

I. What Is In This Root List.

Since no book of reasonable size and moderate
price could give a list of every Russian root mor-
pheme, and since many of those root morphemes occur
in one or two words only, it has been necessary to
choose the more important and useful items. Such a
choice has been based partially upon my intuition
after teaching Russian for 20 years, since no full
study of Russian roots and their frequency exists.
Suggestions for inclusion or omission in the third
edition will be most welcome.

The following have in general been excluded:
1. recent borrowings such as автобус and агроном;
2. most items which are borrowed and have essentially
the same form in Russian and English, e.g., гео-,
математ-, магнит-; 3. a number of roots which form
only nouns and adjectives derived from nouns, e.g.,
ботва, ботвинник, ботвинья. For some words, there is
nothing of pedagogical interest to say, and the root
is omitted from the list. An example is лужа "puddle." Such words may of course be looked up in an
etymological dictionary.

The list in general gives a basic form for the
root and assumes that the user will know the various
predictable changes that roots undergo when made into
words. For reference, a summary of the more important changes is given below. When a change is not
predictable, I have tried to include the variants in
the list. There is a very fine line between giving
insufficient information and giving excess information. In either case, the student does not gain the
maximum. Comments from users will be greatly appre-
ciated, as mentioned above.

II. Roots

A. Some Conventions.

Roots will be written with a hyphen after them
to indicate that a suffix must be added to make a
word. Prefixes will be followed by a hyphen, and
suffixes will be preceded by one. If more than one
prefix or suffix is present, they will be separated
by hyphens: про-из-вод-и-тель. For convenience a
suffix will normally be written with its nom. sg.
ending, as in записка (за-пис-ка), but when it is
desirable to specify the stem of a word, a plus sign
will be placed after the stem: записк+ is the stem of
записка and записа+ is the stem of the verb записать.

11

Where the separation of the word into constituent parts is irrelevant, the hyphens will be omitted, as in the examples just listed.

A *non-syllabic root* is one with no vowel between the consonants. Examples are: жд-, сл-, бр-, жг-. Historically these roots contained the vowels ь or ъ, and most of them have related forms with a vowel, e.g., ожидать, пересылать, наберу, поджог.

A colon (:) following a root refers you to another form of the same root or a related root. The arrows (←, →) mean "comes from, goes to." In definitions of roots, a comma separates synonyms for one meaning, whereas a semi-colon sets off different meanings of one root. Exponential numbers indicate different roots having the same phonemic shape: чин-[1] rank, order, *ord-* чин-[2] make, do, cause; fix чин-[3]: чн-. The letters *ChSl* after a root mean that it is from Church Slavic and shows the characteristics such roots show (see section E below). An asterisk indicates a reconstructed form, such as о-круж-и-ть from *о-круг-и-ть, or a non-occurring form, such as English *drinked.

Definitions given in *spaced italics* indicate word parts from other languages (usually Latin, Greek, or French) used in making *calques*. A calque is a "loan-translation," where the parts of a foreign word are translated one by one using native elements. Thus под-пис-ка can be rendered by *sub-scrip-tion* better than by "under-writ-ing," and со-времен-ный comes out much better as *con-tempor-ary* than as "with-timely." In actual historical fact, of course, it is the other way around: English has normally borrowed a word like *subscription* with minor changes, whereas Russian created a calque by translating the Latin elements into Slavic elements. For a student trying to guess the meaning of unknown Russian words, the process is essentially reversed into a calquing of the English word by using the Latin and other italicized elements to recreate the original model of the Russian word.

Unpaired consonant means one of the six which occur either hard or soft only: ш, ж, ц are always hard, ч, щ, й (/j/) are always soft. Remember that /j/ can also be spelled with a "soft vowel letter" after a vowel, a soft or hard sign, or # (a space): моя́ is /mojá/, made by adding the fem. sg. ending -*a* to the masc. sg. мой /moj/; воробе́й /vorobej/ is like оте́ц /oṭéc/, воробья́ /vorobjá/ is like отца́ /otcá/; яд is /jad/. *Paired consonant* refers to all of the other Russian consonants, which occur in hard-soft pairs: мат "mate" (in chess); мать "mother"; мят

12

"rumpled"; мять "rumple" are, respectively, /mat,
maţ, m̡at, m̡aţ/, where м and т appear hard and soft.

B.   The Shape of Roots.

    Russian roots normally have one syllable and are
of the fixed shape CVC, where the first C stands for
any Russian consonant or certain groups of two or
three consonants, V represents any Russian vowel, and
the final C is one or two *hard* paired consonants.
The final C may also be the single unpaired consonant
/j/, spelled й. Thus ход-, нов-, нёс-, край-,
страд-, блеск-, знай-, ед- (/jed-/) are typical Russian roots. The final consonant or pair of consonants does not usually contain a soft consonant or
one of the five unpaired consonants other than /j/:
ш, ж, ч, щ, ц. Thus паш-, реж-, печь, пищ-, клик-,
новь, вопль are not roots. They are derived from the
roots пах-, рез-, пёк-, пит-, клик-, нов-, and воп-.
    Certain variations from the shape CVC occur.
The first C or the V may be zero, but not in the same
root: ук-, алк-, ид-, бд-, мр-, жм- are all roots,
but *д-, *в-, *й- would not be. The final C is never
missing (except when it has been lost before a suffix
beginning with a consonant; see C2 below), thus *да-,
*ве-, *писа- could not be roots. Some roots have two
syllables, usually of the shape CVRVC, where the
medial R stands for р or л: город-, берег-, холод-,
молок-. In most cases, but not all, a parallel *ChSl*
root of one syllable occurs: град-, брег-, хлад-,
млек-. Other roots with two syllables are usually,
but not always, derivatives of roots with one syllable. In a few cases, I have listed roots ending in a
soft or unpaired consonant (other than /j/) when
positing a hard paired C seemed artificial and of no
pedagogical value, e.g., вещ-, ключ-, кож-, конь-.
The student's working assumption must be that all
roots end in a hard paired consonant or й, since
about 99% do.

C.   Changes in the Shape of Roots.

1.   Mutation of Final Consonant.

    Before suffixes beginning with /j/ (see list of
suffixes) and in a number of other situations, consonants undergo mutation as shown in this table:

13

original C:	п	б	м	ф	в	т	д	с	з
result of mutation :	пль	бль	мль	фль	вль	ч[1]	ж[1]	ш	ж

original C:	ст	ск	ц	к	г	х	н	р	л
result of mutation :	щ	щ	ч	ч	ж	ш	нь	рь	ль

[1] In *ChSl* roots, т goes to щ and д to жд: град- to ограждать, врат- to отвращать (except that д goes to ж in the 1st sg. present/future of verbs: ограж́у).

Examples of mutation of final consonant: *дух-ja to душа, *кап-ja to капля, *по-тер-ja to потеря, *бог-ат-jØ to богач, *воп-jØ to вопль. A final velar consonant (к, г, х) will mutate before a front vowel (и, е, ё) or the soft sign, giving the same results listed above: о-круг-и-ть → окружить, велик-ейший → величайший (cf. новейший) сек+ёт → сечёт, брак-ьный → брачный. Note that the ь of the suffix drops out after the velar has mutated: брак-ьный → брачный. Under certain conditions, primarily in the noun suffix -ьство and the adjective suffix -ьский, the ь does not drop, but becomes е instead: человек-ьство → человечество, человек-ьский → человеческий. The combination ке (but not кё) becomes ча: новейший but величайший, молк- → молчать but сид- → сидеть. For details consult Townsend or other books listed in the *Bibliography*.

A final к will change to ц under certain rather complicated and not always consistent conditions. Examples are: лик- → лицо, рек- → отрицать. In analyzing roots which seem to end in ц, always look for an underlying к.

A final к or г will combine with the noun and verb suffixes -ть to form a -чь: мог-ть → мочь (infinitive, "to be able"), мог-ть → мочь (noun, "power, might"). The infinitive is like лезть, красть, and the noun is like смерть, власть (←влад-ть). In *ChSl* words, кть or гть → -щ-, e.g., помощь (noun, "help").

Before a suffix beginning with ь, the consonant л will become soft and the ь will be kept to show the softness of the consonant: мыло → мыльный. This will sometimes be the case with other consonants: бор-ьба → борьба. The consonants т and д in *ChSl* roots will sometimes mutate to щ and жд before the ь: сут-ьство → существо (but при-сут-ьствие keeps the т: присутствие), обт-ьство → общество, род-ьство →

рождество.

2. Loss of Final or Initial Consonant.

Final м, н, в, й will normally be lost before any consonant other than /j/: стан-ть → стать, жив-ть → жить, знай-ть → знать, but лов-ja → ловля. If the м or н is the second consonant of a root without a vowel (a *non-syllabic* root), it will be replaced by я/a when lost: мн-ть → мять, раз-пн-ть → распять, жм-ть → жать, жн-ть → жать, па-мн-ть → память.

Final т or д will be lost before л: вёд-л → вёл, мёт-л → мёл; before -т- they become с: вёд-ти → вести, мёт-ти → мести, влад-ть → власть, завид-ть → зависть. In the infinitive of two verbs б also changes to с before т: грёб-ти → грести, скрёб-ти → скрести.

Final г, б, д, п may be lost before the verbal suffix -ну-² (the perfective -ну-): двиг-ну-ть → двинуть, за-гб-ну-ть → загнуть, кид-ну-ть → кинуть, за-сп-ну-ть → заснуть. When к or т is the second consonant in a group, loss occurs: блеск-ну-ть → блеснуть, вёрт-ну-ть → вернуть.

Final -ов- (also spelled -ев-) changes to -уй- before vowels (most commonly when the verbal suffix -а- is lost): ков-а+у → кую (куй-у), плёв-а+у → плюю (плюй-у), чист-о-плёв-ьство → чистоплюйство.

Initial в- may be lost when a prefix ends in -б-: обвяз-а-ть → обязать, об-влад-ть → область, but sometimes the в- is kept, and pairs of words may result. In such cases, the form retaining the в- has the more literal meaning: compare обвязать "tie around" and обязать "oblige," or обвить "wind around" and обить "upholster."

Initial /j/ is occasionally lost after a prefix, as in об-ед-∅ → обед (/ob-jed-/ → /obed/), but this is exceptional. The /j/ normally remains: об-ясн-и-ть → объяснить (/ob-jasn-i-t̡/ → /objasn̡it̡/).

3. Change of ё to е.

When a root containing ё acquires a soft suffix, the ё goes to е: чёрн-ь → чернь, пёк-ть → печь.

4. Change of о to а in the Imperfective.

When a verb containing the vowel о in the root gets the imperfectivizing suffix -ывай/-ивай+ the о of the root usually changes to а: про-говор-и+ → про-говар-ивай+, за-мот-ай+ → за-мат-ывай+.

5. Insertion of ы/и in the Imperfective.

When a verb containing a non-syllabic root is imperfectivized, the vowel /i/ (spelled ы or и) will be inserted in the root. This insertion is not affected by the presence or absence of a suffix: за-жг+ → за-жиг-ай+, на-бр-а+ → на-бир-ай+, у-мр+ → у-мир-ай+, за-мк-ну+ → за-мык-ай+, за-с(п)-ну+ → за-сып-ай+. Note how the dropped consonant reappears in the last example. A loose rule for predicting whether ы or и will appear is to use и before н and р, ы elsewhere. This rule has some exceptions, and in a number of roots the presence of и is dictated by the preceding consonant: на-чн+ → на-чин-ай+, за-жм+ → за-жим-ай+. If one pays attention to whether the non-syllabic roots contain ъ or ь, then the presence of ы or и is completely predictable: ы is used when the root has ъ, and и is used when the root has ь: мьр-/мирай+, съп-/сыпай+, мък[1]/мыкай+, etc.

6. Fill Vowels.

Non-syllabic roots will insert fill vowels under certain conditions. An exact statement of these conditions would be quite complicated, but the most common situation is before suffixes and endings without vowels: жг-ть → жчь → жечь, зл-∅+∅ (i.e. zero suffix and zero ending = nom. masc. sg. short form) → зол, лг-ь+∅ (i.e., the suffix ь [= mutation] plus zero ending for nom. sg.) → ложь, gen. лг-ь+и → лжи.

A rule of thumb for determining which vowel to insert is: 1. *after* к, г, х always insert о (угл+∅ → угол, кух-ня → gen. pl. кухонь); 2. *before* р, л, м, н insert ё (е when unaccented): сестра → сестёр, мётла → мётёл → метел, нóжны → нóжен or ножны́ → ножóн. Exception: some monosyllables take о: сн+∅ → сон, по-сл+∅ → посол 3. *before* soft consonant or ц use е: деревня → деревень, отц+∅ → отец; 4. *before* hard consonants (mostly к) use о: сын-к+∅ → сынок, чай-к+∅ → чаёк (/čajók/). Note that these rules must be applied in order, so rule 1 gives us угол before rule 2 could give us *угёл. In the same way, rule 1 gives us кухонь before rule 3 can give *кухень, and rule 2 gives сестёр before rule 4 can give *сестор. In verbs the fill vowel /o/ is spelled only ё, never о: жг-л+∅ → жг → жёг, про-чт-л+∅ → про-чл → прочёл.

When a suffix begins with a soft or hard sign (ь or ъ), a vowel will normally appear in a non-syllabic root: по-сл-ьство → посольство.

7. Vowel Alternations.

Russian roots often show two or more forms which are differentiated from each other by a change of the root vowel (or its disappearance). Thus бр- "take" also appears in the forms бор-, бёр-, бир-, and вёд- "lead" also appears as вод- and вад-. Historically these changes are due to the phenomenon called *ablaut* or *apophony*, which is also responsible for English *sing, sang, sung, song*. Describing all the possible types of ablaut in Russian and describing their occurrence would be much too complicated for this summary, but the following types should be noted:

ё ∿ о: вёд- ∿ вод-[1]   ё ∿ ∅: тём- ∿ тьм-

е ∿ а: лез-[1]∿ лаз-   о ∿ ∅: бор-[2]∿ бр-

о ∿ а: гор-[1]∿ гар-(разгар)   и ∿ ∅: бий- ∿ бьй- (бью =

е ∿ о: дел-[2]∿ дол-[2]   /b̦ij- ∿ b̦j   b̦ju)

ы ∿ о: вый- ∿ вой-[2]   ∅ ∿ и: на-бр-а+ ∿ на-бир-ай+

у ∿ ы: дух- ∿ дых-   ∅ ∿ ы: на-зв-а+ ∿ на-зыв-ай+

To some extent it is possible to predict which vowel will occur in various situations. See the books listed in the *Bibliography* for details.

When the root is of the город- type, a fairly complicated set of alternations may occur. The most common type is: ворот- ∿ верёт- ∿ вёрт- (в́орот, веретен́о, вер[т]н́уть) with *ChSl* врат- and врет- (разврат, вр́емя from *врет-мен-, or more precisely, *vert-men-∅).

One or more of the above types may be combined to produce a series of related forms, such as зв- ∿ зов- ∿ зыв-, дух- ∿ дых- ∿ дох-, мр- ∿ мёр- ∿ мор-[1] ∿ мир-[2], гор-[1] ∿ гар- ∿ гр-ей- ∿ жар-(← *гер-; see C1).

8. Consonant Alternations.

Certain consonants alternate at the end of roots. Roots ending in й frequently have an alternate form in в and vice-versa: грей- ∿ грев-, вий- ∿ вив-, крой-[2] ∿ крый- ∿ кров-[2]. The consonants й and в sometimes alternate with н: дев-[2] ∿ ден-, стой-[1] ∿ стан- ∿ став-. In a few roots -ст and -ск alternate: пуст- ∿ пуск-, блест- ∿ блеск-.

D. Related Roots.

From the materials in part C it is clear that the relationships between roots in Russian are varied and often quite complicated. It is however easy to

learn the various related roots and their differences
in meaning, since related roots almost always begin
with the same consonant (except for a few cases where
a velar and a hushing consonant interchange, e.g.,
гор-[1] ∿ жар-, кон- ∿ чн-). By simply reading through
the list of roots beginning with any given letter one
can find the connections, although the exact nature
of the relationship will not always be obvious without considerable training in Slavic linguistics. Examples of this complexity are блед- ∿ бел- ∿ блёк- ∿
блеск- ∿ блест- ∿ блист-   or бд- ∿ буд- ∿ блюд- ∿
бод(р)-. In view of the fact that, on the one hand,
related roots can be extracted easily from the list
and can thus be seen with their various meanings,
and, on the other, the relationships are often so
complicated as to have no pedagogical value, it
seemed better not to waste several pages giving complete lists of related roots. Comments from users
will be welcome and will be considered in preparing
the third edition.

   For a thorough explanation of related roots a
good etymological dictionary, such as Vasmer (see the
Bibliography), is necessary. Most students will find
many of these etymologies to be of considerable interest, and they will also be surprised to find out
how many Russian words have English cognates.

E.   Church Slavic Elements.

   Many prefixes, roots, and suffixes in Russian
have two slightly different forms. Usually one of
these forms refers to everyday ideas and objects,
whereas the other refers to a more elevated or figu-
rative concept. An example is выворачивать "turn
inside out, unscrew, twist" as opposed to извращать
"pervert, misconstrue" (i.e., turn figuratively inside out). The first word is constructed entirely
of Russian elements, the second entirely of Church
Slavic elements (except for the infinitive suffix
-ть, which is the same for both):

	prefix	root	mutation of -C-	imperfective suffix
Russian	вы-	ворот-	ч	-ивай+
ChSl	из-	врат-	щ	-ай+

   Three important features distinguish *ChSl* roots
from Russian roots:
1. Russian has ё, *ChSl* has e: нёбо "palate of the
   mouth," небо "sky" (the idea in both cases is an
   arching vault over something).

18

2. Russian mutates т to ч and д to ж, *ChSl* mutates т to щ and д to жд: вывора́чивать vs. извраща́ть above, перегора́живать "partition off, block off something" vs. прегражда́ть "bar, block, hinder" (i.e., block off figuratively from something).

3. Russian and Church Slavic have differing combinations of vowels and the consonants р or л. These fall into five types only:

a. R -оро- = *ChSl* -ра-: город- ∿ град-[2], ворот- ∿ врат-
b. R -ере- = *ChSl* -ре-: берег- ∿ брег-, дерев- ∿ древ-
c. R -оло- = *ChSl* -ла-: холод- ∿ хлад-, голов- ∿ глав-
d. R -оло- = *ChSl* -ле-: молок- ∿ млек-, полон- ∿ плен-
(Note that R -оло- corresponds to both -ла- and -ле- in *ChSl*, although -ла- is much more common.)
e. R ро- (initially) = *ChSl* ра-: роз- ∿ раз-[2], ров- ∿ рав-

For more detailed information on Church Slavic elements in Russian, see Townsend, p. 54-60, or one of the books listed in the *Bibliography*.

III. Prefixes and Suffixes

A. Verbal Prefixes.

в-   in, into, *in-, im-, en-, intro*: вводи́ть *introduce*, вписа́ть *inscribe*

вз-   1. up, upward: взойти́ go up, rise; 2. begin an action suddenly: вскрича́ть cry out

воз-   *ChSl* form of вз-, has additional meaning of renewal, repetition, *re-*: воспроизводи́ть reproduce

вы-   (prefix is always stressed in perfective, not in imperfective) 1. out, *ex-*: вы́лететь fly out; 2. to the end, successfully, completely: вы́гореть burn down, burn to ashes

до-   1. action up to a certain point: догна́ть overtake; 2. completion of an action (i.e., getting to the end point): допи́ть finish drinking, drink up; 3. add to, do more of: доли́ть pour more in, add to a liquid by pouring; 4. see недо-

за-   1. begin (usually lacks paired impf.): запла́кать break into tears; 2. action which goes beyond a goal or specified point: заки́нуть throw behind or beyond; 3. cover, block off, close: заде́лать close, block up; 4. action performed in passing: заходи́ть drop in on, stop off while passing

из-   1. *ChSl* equivalent of вы-: исходи́ть come out of, proceed from; 2. to an extreme degree, to exhaustion: износи́ть wear out; исписа́ть fill up with writing

на-	1. on, onto: намазать spread on, smear on; 2. do in (great) quantity: настричь shear a lot, shear a quantity of; 3. (in combination with reflexive particle) get one's fill of, do to satiety: наглядеться look one's fill, get an eyeful of
над-	1. over, *super*-: надзирать oversee, *supervise* 2. do superficially, touch only the surface: надкусить nibble
недо-	do to an insufficient degree, do less than has been expected: недооценить underestimate, недостроенный unfinished, not completely built
низ-	*ChSl* down, downward: низводить bring down, lead down
о-, об-	1. (sur-)round, *circum*-: обнять embrace, обходить go around; 2. factitive (with suffix -и+): освоить master, assimilate, объяснить explain, make clear; 3. (with reflexive) do something badly or in a wrong way: ослышаться hear wrong, оговориться make a slip in speaking
от-	1. away, forth: отходить go away; 2. response, recompense: ответить (speak in response); 3. completion: отделать finish, trim
пере-	1. across, from one place to another, *trans*-: переходить cross over, go across; 2. beyond a limit, too much, in excess: переплатить overpay; 3. again, anew, *re*-: переписать rewrite, copy
по-	1. simple perfective: побелеть become white; 2. do a little: поговорить talk a little, have a short talk; 3. (with suffix -ывай+) do from time to time: помахивать wave from time to time
под-	1. beneath, below, *sub*-: подвергнуть *subject*; 2. motion upwards from under: поднять lift, raise; 3. approach, go up to, proximity: подходить approach; 4. underhand action: подделывать counterfeit; 5. slightly, to a slight degree: подсушить dry a little
пре-	*ChSl* see пере-
пред-	*ChSl* fore, before, in front of, in advance: предсказать foretell
при-	1. up to, against, *ad*-: приковать chain to, fasten to; 2. accompaniment: припев refrain
про-	through, past, by, *pro*-: проехать ride through, ride past/by (+ мимо)
раз-	1. *dis*-: apart, scatter: разогнать disperse; 2. intensely, to a high degree: расспросить interrogate, расхвалить lavish praise; 3. un-, action negated, *dis*-: разлюбить cease to love,

stop loving; 4. progressive increase: разду-
вать fan, blow, rouse

с-   1. together, with, *con-*: сплетать weave to-
      gether, plait; 2. off of, from the top of,
      away: скинуть throw off, слезть get down from,
      dismount

у-   1. away, off, *ab-*: урезать cut off, увезти
      abduct 2. achievement of purpose: усмотреть
      perceive, discover; 3. (with suffix -и+) fac-
      titive: укрепить strengthen, усвоить master,
      learn; 4. lessening (really a subdivision of
      1.): убывать decrease (= become less)

Remember that any prefix may have simple perfective
meaning for a greater or lesser number of verbs,
e.g., написать, прочитать, сделать.

   Most or all prefixes may also have factitive
meaning, but о- and у- are by far the most common.
Some examples with other prefixes are: возвеличить
glorify (= make great), вышколить train, засекретить
make secret, намагнитить magnetize, понизить lower.

   For a fuller discussion of verbs, see Townsend,
Russian Word Formation, or Unbegaun, *Russian Grammar*.
The best treatment is in Isačenko's Грамматический
строй русского языка, II (see the *Bibliography*).

B. Verbal Suffixes.

1. Aspect Suffixes.

-ай+[1]   (always accented) imperfective from prefixed
          perfective отвечай+ ← ответи+, отвращай+ ←
          отврати+

-вай+   (always accented) imperfective from prefixed
          perfective надевай+ ← наден+, подогревай+ ←
          подогрей+

-ывай+   (never accented) imperfective from prefixed
          perfective записывай+ ← записа́+, отворачивай+
          ← отвороти+

-ну+[2]   (-ну+ may be accented or unaccented, it does
          not drop in past) 1. do something quickly, or
          simply do something one time: прыгну+ spring,
          резну+ cut; 2. make a sound X (normally paired
          with an impf. verb in -ай+) ахну+ (ахай+) ex-
          claim, gasp, say "ah!", чихну+ (чихай+) sneeze

   Note that in verbal nouns, -ну- may sometimes
change to -нов-: ис-чез-ну+ → исчезновение. Such
forms are *ChSl*. This applies to both -ну-[1] and -ну-[2].

2. Other Suffixes.

-а+   verbs from roots: писа+ write плака+ cry
-ай+[2] verbs from nouns and other parts of speech:

делай+ ← дело, ахай+ gasp, exclaim, say "ah!"

-e+   1. be in a state of X (stative): сиде+ be sitting, be in a state of sitting, лежа+ (← лёг-, see #C1 above) lie, be lying; 2. make a noise: шуме- make noise, скрипе+ creak, храпе+ snore, пища+ squeak (писк- squeak, squeal)

-ей+   (almost always accented) become X, appear X: белей+ become white, appear white

-и+   1. factitive: бели+ make white, whiten, черни+ blacken; 2. causative: -ложи+ lay (cause to lie)

-ничай+ (also -ичай+, ← [н]ик-ей+) be X, play the role of X, work as X: лодырничай+ be idle, loaf, кокетничай+ be/play the role of a coquette, кухарничай+ work as a cook

-ну+[1] (imperfective, -ну+ drops in past, accent always on stem) become something, get into some state: мёрзну+ freeze, крепну+ become strong

-o+   verbs from roots (only 5 verbs, historically is part of root): коло+ stab, поро+ rip, slash

-ова+   (spelling variant: -ева+, extended forms: -изова+, -ирова+, -изирова+) verbs from foreign words and some native words and roots: ночевать spend the night, интриговать intrigue, нормализовать normalize, нокаутировать knock out, вульгаризировать vulgarize

C. Noun Prefixes and Suffixes.

1. Noun Prefixes.

Prefixation is much less important in the formation of nouns than it is in verbs, even though the number of separate prefixes in nouns is slightly higher. Most nouns with prefixes are derived from verbs by suffixation.

Noun prefixes may be divided into two groups: those of foreign origin and those of Slavic origin. A large number of the foreign prefixes have been borrowed with the words they occur in, but most of them have some degree of productivity within Russian. Many of the Slavic prefixes serve to make calques from foreign words.

a. Foreign Prefixes.

a-   *a-*, without, deprived of: аморальный, аполитичность

анти-   *anti-*: антифашист

архи-   *arch-*: архимошенник super-swindler, super-scoundrel, архиепископ

вице-   *vice-*: вице-консул

22

гипер-	*hyper-*: гиперактивность
де-	(дез- before vowels) *de-*, *dis-*: демилитариза- ция, денационализация, дезинфекция, дезориен- тация
диз- and дис- = де-/дез-	дисквалификация, дизассоци- ация
контр-	*contra-*, *counter-*: контратака, контрпредложение
обер-	over-, chief, super-: обер-прокурор chief prosecutor, обер-жулик, обер-плут super-cheat, super-swindler
про-	1. for, *pro-*: профашист; 2. in place of, *pro-*: проректор
прото-	*proto-*: протозвёзды, прототип
псевдо-	*pseudo-*: псевдонаука
ре-	*re-*: реконструкция, реэвакуация
суб-	*sub-*: субинспектор, субтропики
супер-	*super-*: суперактивность
ультра-	*ultra-*: ультраконсерватор, ультракороткий
экс-	*ex-*: (in two meanings: "out" and "former") экспатриация, экс-чемпион

b. Slavic Prefixes.

без-	without, *dis-*: безделье idleness, бессоница insomnia, беспорядок disorder
за-	beyond, on the other side of, *trans-*: Забай- калье *Transbajkal*, Закарпатье *Transcarpathia*, загород countryside
между-	between, *meso-*: междуречье *Mesopotamia*, между- горье the area between two mountains
на-	on: нагорье upland, наушники earflaps; head- phones
над-	*super-*, over, above: надсмотр *supervision*, надпись *superscription, inscription*
не-	not, *non-*, *un-*, *dis-*: недруг enemy, невыгода disadvantage, неправда untruth, неудача fail- ure, lack of success
пере-	*re-*, secondary: перевыборы election held a second time, пересмена second shift. Most nouns with this prefix are derived from verbs and have the relevant meaning of the verbal prefix.
по-	area along: Поволжье area along the Volga, побережье littoral, sea-coast
под-	under, *sub-*; near: подбородок chin, подвид *subspecies*, подземелье underground, Подмос- ковье area around Moscow, near Moscow, подтро- пики subtropics
пра-	*pre-*, *proto*, great- (in family), = German *ur-*: праязык protolanguage, прадед great grand- father, ancestor

пред-   before, *pre-*: предплечье forearm, предыстория
         prehistory
при-   1. near, adjoining, *sub-*: приморье littoral,
         пригород *suburb*; 2. additional, secondary:
         прирост additional growth, припев refrain,
         chorus, привкус aftertaste, taste mixed in
         with another
про-   partial presence of something, trace of: про-
         золоть flecks of gold, vein of gold, просинь
         bluish tint, прослойка streak, layer
противо- *anti-*, *counter*: противоракета antimissile
         missile, противоток countercurrent, contraflow
раз-   indicates a high degree of something (collo-
         quial): раскрасавица very beautiful woman,
         растуманы very thick fog, расподлец scoundrel
         of the worst sort
сверх-   *super-*: сверхчеловек superman
со-   (less often с-) with, *co-*, *con-*: соавтор co-
         author, сотрудник *collaborator*, спутник
         fellow-traveller, satellite

2. Noun Suffixes.

The number of noun suffixes is very large, and
many of them have more than one meaning. A full
treatment would require a separate book. The following list attempts to cover only the more common and
important ones, and it does not necessarily give
every possible meaning or variant form. Suffixes
beginning with ь or ъ before a consonant are listed
in alphabetical order as if the ь or ъ were not present: e.g., -ьник is listed under "н".

-а   nouns from roots: плата payment, дума thought,
         тоска yearning
-аж   abstract nouns (mostly borrowings): пилотаж
         pilotage
-ак (also -як) person or thing characterized by the
         root: чудак eccentric, лежак a type of wooden
         bed; a wooden beam left in lying position
-ака   (pejorative) agent: писака scribbler, зевака
         idler
-ант   agent: симулянт simulator, faker, malingerer
-анин   see -янин
-арь   agent: лекарь doctor, пекарь baker
-ат   object or result of an action: адресат addres-
         see, фильтрат filtrate
-атор   agent: реставратор restorer, экзаменатор exam-
         iner
-ач   agent: ткач weaver, рвач self-seeker, grabber
-ьба   deverbal nouns: борьба fight, struggle,
         стрельба shooting, firing

24

-ёж   nouns from verbal roots: грабёж robbery, pillage, платёж payment
-еж   *ChSl* form of preceding: рубеж boundary, line, падеж case ("falling") (Compare Russian падёж "epizootic loss of cattle.")
-ение and -енье   deverbal nouns: курение smoking, печение baking, печенье pastry, cookies
-ёнок   young of animals or persons: зверёнок young animal, волчонок wolf cub, турчонок young Turk, Turkish child
-ент see -ант: адсорбент adsorbent, конкурент competitor
-енька see -онька
-ёр   agent: режиссёр producer, ухажёр suitor
-ец (-ьц)   1. agent: певец singer, борец fighter; 2. nouns from adj. indicating person who possesses quality of adj.: мертвец dead person, мудрец wise man, sage; 3. belonging to some group or movement: марафонец Marathon runner, ленинец Leninist, комсомолец member of the Komsomol; 4. diminutive: хлебец, вопросец
-знь   abstract nouns: жизнь life, боязнь fear
-ие and -ье   collective and abstract nouns: десятилетие decade, бельё linens, white goods, наследие legacy, heritage, доверие faith, confidence
-изм = English -*ism*: ленинизм Leninism
-изна   abstract nouns from adjectives: белизна whiteness, кривизна crookedness
-ик   1. nouns denoting profession or distinguishing characteristic: химик chemist, политик politician, диабетик diabetic, лунатик lunatic, прозаик prose writer; 2. nouns from adjectives, denoting a person or thing who has the quality described by the adjective: старик old man, рыжик orange-agaric (a type of mushroom, *Lactarius deliciosus*), долгоносик person with a long nose; 3. diminutive: слоник, прутик
-ин = -янин: грузин Georgian, эллин Hellene, Greek
-ина   1. object or result of action: царапина scratch, трещина crack; 2. type of meat: свинина pork, солонина salted or corned meat; 3. place: равнина plain, целина virgin lands, быстрина rapids; 4. individual item from a group: соломина single straw, десятина tithe, 1/10; 5. abstract nouns: глубина depth, ширина width, breadth
-иня see -ыня
-ист   = English -*ist*: специалист specialist, славист Slavist
-иха   feminine nouns: повариха cook, волчиха she-wolf

25

ица- 1. abstract nouns: бессоница insomnia, разница difference; 2. feminine nouns: певица singer, львица lioness; 3. diminutives: лужица puddle, водица water

-ич 1. inhabitant of some place: москвич Moscovite серпухович inhabitant of Serpukhov; 2. patronymics: Ильич, Фомич

-ишка (for fem. nouns and masc. animates) and -ишко (for neuter nouns and inanimate masc.) pejorative-diminutive: мальчишка brat, urchin, городишка miserable little town, podunk

-ище 1. place where action takes place or object is located: хранилище storehouse, depository, repository, пастбище pasture; 2. augmentative: городище great big city

-ия = English -ion: ревизия revision, инверсия inversion

-ja (-j- causes mutation of last consonant of root where possible) nouns: потеря loss, кража theft, порча spoiling, spoilage, damage

-ька (-ька after к, г, х) 1. deverbal nouns: тёрка grater, стружка shaving(s), чистка cleansing, purge; 2. feminine nouns: студентка female student, таджичка Tadzhik woman; 3. diminutive: головка head (esp. of cabbage, garlic, etc.), горка hill

-ько diminutives: пивко beer, очко pip, point, hole

-ла agent: запевала first singer, надувала swindler, cheat

-лец see -ец[1]: страдалец sufferer

-лина variant of -ина[1]: извалина bend, crook, convolution

-лка agent: сушилка dryer

-ло agent: мыло soap, шило awl, начало beginning

-льник agent: будильник alarm clock

-льщик agent: носильщик porter

-ние and -нье deverbal nouns: писание writing, читание reading, ви́дение vision, sight, враньё fibbing, lies, nonsense

-ьник agent: заступник intercessor, defender, насмешник scoffer, mocker

-ьница 1. place for something: сахарница sugar bowl, гробница tomb, sepulchre; 2. place where action occurs: мельница mill, звонница belfry, виселица gallows

-нье see -ние

-ьня 1. deverbal nouns: стряпня cooking, concoction, резня slaughter; 2. place where action occurs: бойня slaughterhouse, читальня reading-room, спальня bedroom

-ович patronymics: Петрович, Иванович

-овна patronymics: Петровна, Ивановна
-ок (-ёк in most cases) 1. diminutives: городок, чаёк
       (← чай), грибок; 2. agent: едок eater, скребок
       scraper; 3. deverbal nouns: кивок nod, скачок
       jump, зевок yawn; 4. result of verbal action:
       кипяток boiling water, окурок stub or butt of
       cigarette or cigar, обмерок short measure or
       short weight
-онок see -ёнок
-онька and -енька diminutive-affectionate: дедонька
       grandfather, дяденька uncle, рученька hand
-ость abstract nouns from adjectives: мягкость soft-
       ness, пассивность passivity
-ота abstract nouns from adjectives: теплота
       warmth, быстрота swiftness
-ьствие *ChSl* for -ьство: соответствие *correspondence*
-ьство abstract and collective nouns: руководство
       leadership (both as an abstract and as a group
       of people), учительство a) the teaching pro-
       fession, b) teachers (collective), c) teach-
       ing, instruction
-тель agent from verbs: учитель teacher, писатель
       writer
-тие and -тьё deverbal nouns: развитие development,
       житьё life, living
-ток see -ок
-ть nouns, usually abstract: смерть death, власть
       power (← вдад-), печь stove, oven (← пёк-)
-тьё see -тие
-ун agent, with meaning of "inclined to do X, al-
       ways doing X, doing X to excess": лгун liar,
       бегун runner, говорун chatterbox, грызун
       rodent
-ура collective and abstract nouns: аспирантура
       graduate study, graduate students, профессура
       professorship, professorate, диктатура dicta-
       torship
-ушка (for fem. and animate masc.) and -ушко (for
       neuter and inanimate masc.) diminutive-
       affectionate: коровушка, братушка, дядюшка,
       морюшко, хлебушко
-ьце see -ьцо
-ция = English -*tion*: фальсификация, реконструкция
       (normally this suffix has been borrowed with
       the word)
-ьцо (and its unaccented spelling variant -ьце)
       neuter diminutives: словцо, винцо, болотце
-ьчик variant of -ьщик occurring after т, д, с, з, ж
-ьша 1. nouns denoting females as opposed to males:
       секретарша secretary, 2. wife of the person
       denoted by the base noun: генеральша wife of a

general

-ЬЩИК (-ЬЧИК after т, д, с, з, ж; -ИК after -щ-)
    agent: проверщик verifier, checker, controller
    разносщик peddler, hawker, пищик (← писк-)
    reed (in musical instrument), bird-caller

-ЫНЯ   feminine nouns: рабыня female slave, богиня
    goddess, монахиня nun

-ЬШКО   diminutives: горлышко throat, neck (of a
    bottle), солнышко (← солнце)

-Ь   nouns, often abstracts: зелень verdure;
    greens, vegetables; green, чернь riff-raff,
    rabble, mob, связь tie, bond, connection, ложь
    lie, перепись census

-ЯГА   agent, usually carries connotation of doing
    action energetically: работяга hard worker,
    бродяга tramp

-ЯК see -ак

-ЯНИН (-janин) inhabitant of a place, member of a
    group: горожанин city-dweller, гражданин citi-
    zen, киевлянин Kievite, христианин Christian

-ЯТА   forms pl. of nouns with -ёнок in sg.

-∅   (zero suffix) most common meaning is deverbal
    noun: осмотр inspection, survey, examination,
    зов call, summons, evocation

D. Adjective Prefixes and Suffixes.

1. Adjective Prefixes.

    These are in general the same ones used with
nouns. The following are restricted to adjectives:

вне-   outside, *extra-*: внеклассный *extracurricular*,
    внеочередной *extraordinary*

внутри-   inside, *intra-*: внутрипартийный intra-party

до-   *pre-*, before: довоенный pre-war, допетровский
    pre-Petrine

еже-   each, every, -ly: ежемесячный monthly, еже-
    дневный everyday, daily

интер- (in foreign borrowings) *inter-*: интервокальный
    intervocalic

меж-   (variant of между-) located between something,
    inter-: межпланетный *interplanetary*

наи-   superlatives: наиближайший closest, nearest
    наилучший best

не-без- not without, having a certain amount of:
    небезопасный unsafe, insecure, небезуспешный
    not unsuccessful, having some success

около- around, *circum-*: окололунный *circumlunar*,
    окололитературный on the fringes of literature

по-[1]   division into separate units: понедельная зар-
    плата pay by the week

28

по–[2]   = после: посмертный *posthumous*
пре–   *ChSl* very, greatly, most: пресмешной ludicrous
транс– across, *trans-*: транссибирский Transsiberian
чрез–   *ChSl* and через– across, *trans-*: чрезмерный
        excessive, чересседельный across the saddle
экстра– *extra-*: экстралингвистический *extralinguis-*
        tic

2. Adjective Suffixes.

Only the more frequent and important are listed here, since a large number of the other suffixes occur only in a small number of words.

-ав-   кровавый bloody, дырявый full of holes, con-
        taining holes
-аст-   distinguished by the item named, having a lot of
        it: зубастый having a lot of large teeth,
        toothy, грудастый large-bosomed
-ат-   possessing thing named: зубатый having teeth,
        dentate, женатый married (of a man)
-ейший superlative, having the characteristic to a
        high degree: новейший newest, very new, вели-
        чайший greatest, great
-енький affectionate-diminutive: хорошенький, моло-
        денький
-ий   (stem: -j-) possessive: вдовий (fem. вдовья)
        widow's, казачий Cossack, рыбий fish's, коро-
        вий cow's, bovine
-ин-[1] possessives from nouns in -а: мамин, сестрин,
        дядин, Иринин, Володин, старостин
-ин-[2] characteristic of the base word: звериный,
        лошадиный
-ист-   characterized by X, having the property of X:
        слоистый having layers, layered, голосистый
        full-voiced, пушистый fuzzy, having a cover
        of down
-к-   adjective, mostly from roots: низкий low,
        жидкий liquid
-ьлив- characterized by X, having X: дождливый rainy,
        талантливый talented
-ьн-   the most common adjective suffix in Russian,
        over half of all adjectives are made with
        -ьн-: водный, рыбный, интересный, речной
        (← река)
-ьнь-   adjectives of time or position or relation:
        летний summer, передний front, forward, брат-
        ний brother's
-ов-[1] possessives: дедов, братов, царёв, Сергеев,
        Иванов
-ов-[2] классовый pertaining to social classes, тигро-
        вый tiger-, tiger's

29

-оват- having the characteristic to an attenuated
       degree: слабоватый weakish, синеватый bluish
-ьск- primarily, but not exclusively, adjectives
       from proper or place names: ленинский Lenin-
       ist, ленинградский pertaining to Leningrad,
       рижский pertaining to Riga, американский Amer-
       ican, городской city-, municipal, университет-
       ский university-
-яв-   see -ав-
-ян-   made of or containing something: ржаной rye,
       серебряный silver

BIBLIOGRAPHY

This bibliography is intended to give some suggestions for further reading, but is only a beginning. For a detailed bibliography, see Dean S. Worth, *A Bibliography of Russian Word-Formation* (Slavica, 1977).

A. Grammars of Russian

Исаченко, А. В.: Грамматический строй русского языка, Морфология, I^2, 1965, II, 1960, SAV, Bratislava. Probably the best single book for verbal prefixes, but does not contain much on suffixal word formation in nouns and adjectives.

Isačenko, A. V.: *Die Russische Sprache der Gegenwart, Teil I, Formenlehre*, Halle, 1962. A reworked version of the preceding, somewhat less thorough but directed specifically toward German-speaking students. Since English is a Germanic language, this version will contain some useful information not in the Russian version, which is designed for Slovak-speaking students.

Шведова, Н. Ю., ред.: Грамматика современного русского литературного языка, Moscow, 1970. Somewhat more up-to-date in methodology than the Vinogradov grammar (below), but still leaves a lot to be desired.

Unbegaun, B. O.: *Russian Grammar,* Oxford Univ. Press, 1957. Concise but excellent descriptions of prefixes and suffixes.

Виноградов, В. В., ред.: Грамматика русского языка, том I, Moscow, 1952 (reprinted 1960). Ponderous and poor on analysis, but with lots of examples.

B. Works on Word Formation

Norbury, J. K. W., *Word Formation in the Noun and Adjective,* Cambridge Univ. Press, 1967.

Потиха, З. А.: Современное русское словообразование, Moscow, 1970. Has a useful bibliography on pages 375-382.

Шанский, Н. М.: Очерки по русскому словообразованию, Moscow, 1968.

Townsend, C. E.: *Russian Word-Formation,* McGraw-Hill, New York, 1968, corrected reprint, Slavica, 1975. The best work available in English, and on some subjects the best available in any language. Also contains a description of the one-stem system for verbs.

C. Root Lists

Patrick, G. Z.: *Roots of the Russian Language,* Pit-
man, New York, 1938. Short but useful.

Wolkonsky, C. and M. A. Poltoratzky: *Handbook of Russian Roots,* Columbia Univ. Press, New York, 1961.
Gives examples of words and their use. No concept
of conditioned alternants of roots. Primitive.

Worth, D. S. et al.: *Russian Derivational Dictionary,*
Elsevier, New York, 1970. Segmentation of about
100,000 words into roots and affixes. Very useful, although it gives no meanings and its idea of
what constitutes a root is sometimes subject to
argument. Since I obtained a copy of this book
only after my own was essentially finished, it has
not been used much in the preparation of *Russian
Root List.*

D. Dictionaries Concerned with Roots, Etymologies, etc.

Bielfeldt, H. H.: *Rückläufiges Wörterbuch der russis-
chen Sprache der Gegenwart,* Berlin (East), 1965[2].
A reverse-order dictionary of Russian which can be
used to compare words with a given suffix. Can be
used without any knowledge of German.

Цыганенко, Г. П.: Этимологический словарь русского
языка, Kiev, 1970. Designed for secondary-school
teachers and students in the USSR.

Morris, W., ed.: *The American Heritage Dictionary of
the English Language,* Houghton Mifflin, New York,
1969. Contains the best and most up-to-date etymologies for English words, with an appendix of
Indo-European roots which will help to connect
material from Russian etymological dictionaries
(such as Vasmer, Shanskij, and Cyganenko) with
English words.

Потиха, З. А.: Школьный словообразовательный словарь,
Moscow, 1964. Very traditional. Consists of word
list in alphabetical order with words broken up by
slashes. Some useful appendices.

Шанский, Н. М. и др.: Краткий этимологический словарь
русского языка, second edition, Moscow, 1972.
Addressed to secondary-school use in the USSR.
Not always reliable.

Vasmer, M.: *Russisches etymologisches Wörterbuch,* 3
volumes, Heidelberg, 1953-1958. A superb etymological dictionary which supersedes all previous
works. A Russian translation in 4 volumes, with
some additions and a few deletions by O. N. Truba-
čev, has appeared in Moscow under the title Этимологический словарь русского языка, vol. I, 1964;

vol. II, 1967; vol. III, 1971, vol. IV, 1973.

Vasmer, M. et al.: *Russisches rückläufiges Wörterbuch,* 2 volumes, Heidelberg, 1958-9.   A somewhat
larger and much more expensive reverse-order
dictionary than Bielfeldt (see above).

Тихонов, А. Н.: Школьный словообразовательный словарь
русского языка. Пособие для учащихся.   Moscow,
1978.   Takes a base word and gives derivatives
from it, rather than dealing with roots, but has
a lot of useful material.

Persons who wish to carry their studies further are
especially urged to look at the various publications
of A. I. Kuznecova (see the *MLA Bibliography* and the
bibliography Славянское языкознание, published in
Moscow; the more recent volumes each cover a period
of five years).   Further bibliography for works
published after the cut-off of Worth's bibliography
can be found in Kuznecova's works and in the two
bibliographies just mentioned above.   This material
is primarily of a theoretical nature, rather than
pedagogical.

АЛ–	scarlet		БИР–	: бр-
АЛК–	hunger; greed		БЛАГ–	*ChSl* good, bless, welfare
БАВ–	add; amuse (caus. ← быв-)		БЛЁВ–	vomit
БАЙ–	tell, speak, say; sing		БЛЕД–	pale
			БЛЕЙ–	bleat
БАЛ–	spoil, indulge		БЛЁК–	pale, fade
БАР–	noble, gentle, lord		БЛЕСК–	sparkle, shine, glitter
БАСН–	tale, fable (← бай)		БЛЕСТ–	: блеск-
			БЛИЗ–	near, close, *proxi-*
БД–	awake, alert, vigilant		БЛИСТ–	: блест-
БЕГ–	run, flee, *fuge*		БЛУД–	roam, wander, lose one's way; sin
БЕД–	trouble, misfortune; poverty; conquer, *vic-/vinc-*		БЛЮД–[1]	observe, watch -*vise* : буд-[1]
			БЛЮД–[2]	dish
БЕЛ–	white, *alb-*		БОГ–	riches, lavish; god
БЕР–	: бр-			
БЕРЕГ–	bank, shore, bound, limit		БОГ-АТ–	: бог- rich
			БОД–	butt
БЕРЁГ–	guard, watch, save, preserve		БОД(Р)–	awake, alert, hale, hearty, brisk, cheerful, courage
БЕРЕМ(ЁН)–	(← бр-) load, burden; pregnant			
			БОЙ–[1]	fear
БЕС–	mad, fury, rage; devil, demon		БОЙ–[2]	(← бий-) beat, battle, fight, slaughter; brisk, sharp
БИВ–	: бий			
БИЙ–	beat, strike, hit			

БОК-   side, lateral

БОЛ-[1]   pain, hurt;
         sick, ill

БОЛ-[2]   big, large

БОЛОГ-   : благ-

БОЛОТ-   swamp

БОЛТ-   stir, shake;
         hang, dangle,
         chatter, babble

БОР-[1]   fight, struggle

БОР-[2]   : бр-

БОРОД-   beard

БОРОН-   (← бор-[1]) fight,
         -fend, -fense

БОС-   bare (foot)

БР-   (БЬР-) take,
         -lect

БРАД-   ChSl : бород-

БРАН-[1] scold, abuse,
         curse

БРАН-[2] : борон-

БРАТ-   brother, fratern-,
         fratri-

БРЕГ-   ChSl : берег

БРЁГ-   ChSl : берёг-

БРЁД-   wander, roam; rave

БРЕЗГ-   disgust, squeamish

БРЕЙ-   : брий-

БРЕМ(ЕН)-   ChSl :
         берем(ён)-

БРИЙ-   shave

БРОД-   : бред-

БРОН-   armor

БРОС-   throw, hurl;
         abandon

БРЫЗГ-   splash, splatter,
         sprinkle

БРЮЗГ-   grumble

БУД-[1]   ChSl waken, rouse,
         excite (caus. ←
         бд-)

БУД-[2]   future

БУЙ-   rage, storm, wild,
         violent

БУКВ-   letter, liter-

БУР-   storm

БУХ-   swell, puff up

БЫВ-   be, exist

БЫЙ-   : быв-

БЫСТР-   swift, fast

БЬЙ-   : бий

ВАГ-   weight, esteem,
         importance

ВАД-   : вод-[1]

ВАЛ-   pile up, heap up;
         throw; wave

ВАР-   boil, cook

ВДОВ-   widow

ВЕД-	know	ВЕТХ-	old, decrepit
ВЁД-	lead, *-fer*, *-late*, *-duce*, *-duct*	ВЕЩ-	thing, substance, essence
ВЕЖЛ-	(← вед-) polite	В-ЗА-ИМ-	mutual
ВЁЗ-	convey, carry by vehicle, *-port*, *-fer*, *-duct*	ВИВ-	: вий-
		ВИД-	see, view, vision, form, appearance, *-spect*
ВЕЙ-	blow		
ВЕК-	long time, century, age, life, eternal	ВИЗГ-	squeal, squeak
		ВИЙ-	wind, twist
ВЕЛ-¹	command, order, will	ВИН-¹	guilt, fault, blame, *-cuse*
ВЕЛ-²	great, big	ВИН-²	wine, *vin-*
ВЕР-	faith, trust, believe, true, sure	ВИНТ-	screw, spiral
		ВИР-	: вр-
ВЕРГ-	throw, hurl, *-ject*	ВИС-	: вес-
		ВИСТ-	: вид-
ВЕРЕТ-	: вёрт-	ВИХ-	(← вий-) twist, hurl, throw, wave
ВЕРЗ-	open		
ВЕРСТ-	: верз-	ВКУС-	(← кус-¹) taste
ВЁРТ-	: ворот-	ВЛ-	: вол-
ВЕРХ-	top, upper, surface	ВЛАГ-	moisture, damp
		ВЛАД-	*ChSl* : волод-
ВЕС-	hand, *-pend*; weight	ВЛАК-	*ChSl* : волок-
ВЕСЁЛ-	gay, happy	ВЛАСТ-	: влад-
ВЕСТ-	: вед-	ВЛЁК-	: волок-
ВЕТ-	say, speak	ВН-	(ВЪН-) out, outside
ВЕТР-	(← вей-) wind		
		ВНУТР-	: ← нутр-

36

ВОД-[1]	: вёд-	ВРЕД-	*ChSl* harm, injury, damage
ВОД-[2]	water, marine, *aqua-, hydro-*	ВРЕМ(ЁН)-	time, *temp-, tempor-*
ВОЗ-	: вёз-	ВС-	(ВьС-) all, entire, *omni-*
ВОЙ-[1]	war, military	ВСТРЕТ-	(← рет-) meet
ВОЙ-[2]	: вый-	ВТОР-	second
ВОЛ-	will, free	ВЫГОД-	(← год-) advantage
ВОЛН-	wave, agitation	ВЫВ-	: вый
ВОЛОД-	rule, power, possess, *domin-*	ВЫЙ-	howl
ВОЛОК-[1]	drag, pull, attract; *-tract*	ВЫК-	accustom, custom, habit
ВОЛОК-[2]	wrap, *-velop*	ВЫС-	high, *alt-*
ВОЛХ-	magic	ВЬЙ-	: вий-
ВОН-[1]	smell, stink	ВЯД-	fade
ВОН-[2]	: вн-	ВЯЗ-	bind, tie, join, stick, viscous, adhere, *-nect*
ВОП-	cry out, shout	ВЯЛ-	: вяд-
ВОР-	steal, thief		
ВОРК-	grumble		
ВОРОТ-	turn, *-vert, -vort, -verse, -volve*	ГАД-[1]	guess, divine
ВОСТР-	: остр-	ГАД-[2]	vile, loathsome, nasty, filthy
ВР-	(ВьР-) lie, talk nonsense, fib, garble	ГАР-	: гор-[1]
ВРАГ-	*ChSl* enemy, *enm-, inim-*	ГАС-	extinguish
ВРАЖД-	*ChSl* (← враг-ьд-) : враг-	ГБ-	bend, flexible, supple
		ГД-	(ГъД-) time
ВРАТ-	*ChSl* : ворот-	ГИБ-[1]	: гб-

ГИБ-[2]   perish, ruin,
          destruction,
          variant of гиб-[1]

ГЛАВ-   head; chief,
          principal, *capit-*

ГЛАД-[1] smooth

ГЛАД-[2] *ChSl* : голод-

ГЛАЗ-   eye

ГЛАС-   *ChSl* : голос-

ГЛОТ-   gulp, swallow

ГЛОХ-   : глух-

ГЛУБ-   deep

ГЛУП-   stupid, foolish

ГЛУХ-   deaf, dull;
          remote

ГЛЯД-   look, glance

ГН-[1]   bend (see гб-)

ГН-[2]   drive, chase

ГНЕВ-   anger, wrath

ГНЁТ-   oppress

ГНИЙ-   rot, decay

ГНОЙ-   : гний-

ГНУС-   vile, repulsive,
          shun

ГОВ-   beef, cow

ГОВОР-   talk, speech

ГОД-   (cf. гд-) time,
          year; fitting,
          proper, advanta-
          geous

ГОЛ-   bare, naked

ГОЛОВ-   head

ГОЛОД-   hunger

ГОЛОС-   voice

ГОН-   : гн-[2]

ГОР-[1]   burn, heat; bit-
          ter; woe, grief

ГОР-[2]   (горло)(cf. жр-[1])
          throat, neck

ГОР-[3]   mountain

ГОРБ-   hump, bump, hunch

ГОРД-   proud

ГОРК-   : гор-[1]

ГОРОД-   (град-[2]) enclo-
          sure; town, city,
          civi-; partition,
          barrier, fence;
          garden

ГОРЬК-   : гор-[1]

ГОСПОД-   lord, master,
          domin-

ГОСТ-   guest

ГОТОВ-   ready

ГРАБ-   grab, rob

ГРАД-[1] reward

ГРАД-[2] *ChSl* : город-

ГРАД-[3] hail

ГРАН-   border, edge,
          facet

ГРЁБ-   dig, bury; row;
          comb

38

ГРЕВ- : грей-

ГРЁЗ- dream

ГРЕЙ- (: гор-[1]) heat, warm

ГРЕМ- ring, peal, thunder

ГРЕХ- sin

ГРОБ- (cf. грёб-) grave, coffin

ГРОЗ- storm; threat

ГРОМ-[1] thunder; loud

ГРОМ-[2] mass, huge, enormous

ГРОМ-АД- : гром-[2]

ГРОМОЗД- : гром-[2]

ГРОХ- crash, rumble, rattle

ГРУБ- coarse, rude

ГРУД- chest, breast

ГРУЗ- load, burden

ГРУСТ- sad, melancholy

ГРЫЗ- gnaw

ГРЯД- go, come, walk

ГРЯЗ- dirt, mud, filth

ГРЯН- : гряд-

ГУБ-[1] (cf. гиб-[2]) ruin, destroy

ГУБ-[2] lip

ГУД- hum, buzz; hoot

ГУЛ- stroll

ГУСТ- thick, dense

ДАВ-[1] press, squeeze

ДАВ-[2] long ago, old, former

ДАД- : дай-

ДАЙ- give

ДАЛ- far

ДАЛЁК- : дал-

ДАН- : дай-

ДАР-[1] (← дай-) gift, *don-*

ДАР-[2] (phps. ← др-) strike, hit, blow

ДАТ- : дай

ДАЧ- : дай

ДВ- two

ДВИГ- move, motion

ДВИН- : двиг-

ДВОЙ- two, double, dual, *bi-*

ДВОР- court

ДЕВ-[1] girl, maid

ДЕВ-[2] : ден-

ДЁД- : ден-

ДЕЙ-[1] do, act, work, make

39

ДЕЙ-² : ден-

ДЕЛ-¹ (← дей-¹) make, do, deed, business

ДЕЛ-² divide, share

ДЕН- place, put

ДЕР- : др-

ДЁРГ- hold, pull, -*tain*, -*tention*; tug

ДЕРЕВ- tree, wood

ДЕРЖАВ- (← дёрг-) state, -*crat*

ДЕРЗ- bold, daring, impudent

ДЕТ- child

ДЁШЁВ- cheap

ДИВ- wonder, marvel

ДИК- wild, savage

ДИР- : др-

ДЛ- (ДЪЛ-) long

ДЛИН- : дл-

ДН-¹ (ДЪН-) bottom

ДН-² (ДЬН-) day

ДОБ- time; convenient, fitting

ДОБЛ- valour, valiant

ДОБР- (← доб-) kind, good

ДОВЛ- (← до-вол-) suf-fice, satisfy

ДОЙ- milk

ДОЛ-¹ (← дл-) long, valley

ДОЛ-² (← дел-²?) part, share

ДОЛБ- hollow

ДОЛГ-¹ debt, duty

ДОЛГ-² (← дол-¹) long

ДОН- : дн-¹

ДОР- : др-

ДОРОГ-¹ dear; expensive

ДОРОГ-² road

ДОСТОЙ- (← стой-) worthy

ДОЧ(ЕР)- daughter

ДОХ- : дух-, -*spir*-

ДР- (ДЬР-) tear; fight

ДРАГ- *ChSl* : дорог-¹

ДРАЗ- irritate

ДРЕВ-¹ old, ancient

ДРЕВ-² *ChSl* : дерев-

ДРЕМ- dream, snooze, doze

ДРОБ- split, crush, divide, minute

ДРОВ- : дерев-

ДРОГ- tremble, shudder, shake

ДРУГ-[1] friend, *ami-, amic-*

ДРУГ-[2] other

ДРЯН- rubbish, junk

ДРЯХ(Л)- old, decrepit

ДУВ- : дуй-

ДУГ- bow, arch

ДУЙ- blow

ДУМ- think

ДУР- foolish, stupid, *stup-*; bad

ДУХ- spirit, breath, breathe; close, stuffy

ДЫМ- smoke

ДЫР- (← др-) hole

ДЫХ- : дух-

ЕД-[1] ride

ЕД-[2] eat

ЕД(И)Н- *ChSl* : од(и)н- *uni-*

ЕЗД- : ед-[1], *-gress*

ЁМ- : им-, *cap-*, take

ЕСТ- exist, natural, nature

ЕХ- : ед-[1]

ЖАД- thirst, greed

ЖАЛ-[1] pity, regret; complain

ЖАЛ-[2] (← жм-) sting, bite

ЖАР- heat, hot, fire

ЖВ- : жёв-

ЖГ- burn

ЖД- wait

ЖЁВ- chew

ЖЕЛ- desire, wish

ЖЁЛТ- yellow

ЖЁН- woman, wife, *femin-*

ЖЕР- : жр-[1]

ЖЕРТВ- : жр-[2]

ЖЁСТ- hard, stiff; strict, cruel

ЖИВ- live, *viv-, bio-*

ЖИВОТ- (← жив-) life; animal; stomach

ЖИГ- : жг-

ЖИД-[1] liquid

ЖИД-[2] : жд-

ЖИЛ- : жив-

ЖИМ- : жм-

ЖИН- : жн-

ЖИР-[1] : жр-[1]

41

ЖИР-[2]	fat, grease	ЗВУК-	(← звон-) sound
ЖИТ-[1]	: жив-	ЗД-	(ЗьД-) build, erect, create, *edif-*
ЖИТ-[2]	grain		
ЖМ-	press, squeeze	ЗДОРОВ-	health
ЖН-	reap, harvest	ЗДРАВ-	*ChSl* : здоров-
ЖОГ-	: жг-	ЗЕВ-	yawn
ЖОР-	: жр-[1]	ЗЕЛ-	green
ЖР-[1]	gulp, eat	ЗЕЛЁН-	: зел-
ЖР-[2]	sacrifice	ЗЁМ-	land, earth, ground, *-terr-*, terrestrial
ЗАБАВ-	(← за-бав-) amuse	ЗЕР-	: зр-
ЗАБВ-	: забыв-	ЗЁРН-	grain
ЗАБОТ-	care, worry, concern	ЗИД-	: зд-
		ЗИЙ-	: зев-, gape
ЗАБЫВ-	: (← за-быв-) forget	ЗИМ-	winter
ЗАВИД-	: (← за-вид-) envy	ЗИР-	: зр-
ЗАД-	back, rear	ЗЛ-	(ЗьЛ-) evil, bad, malicious, angry
ЗАКОН-	law, legal		
ЗАР-	(← зр-) dawn, dusk, glow, light	ЗЛАТ-	*ChSl* : золот-
		ЗНАЙ-	know, *cogn-*
ЗВ-	(ЗъВ-) call, evoke, *voc-,-voke*	ЗНАК-	(← знай-) sign, *sign-*
ЗВЕН-	ring, resound; link	ЗНАКОМ-	(← знай-) known
		ЗНАМ(ЁН-)	: (← знай-) sign, banner
ЗВЕР-	animal (wild)		
ЗВОЛ-	(← вол-) permit	ЗОВ-	: зв-
ЗВОН-	ring, resound, sound	ЗОД-	: зд-

42

ЗОЛОТ– gold

ЗОР– : зр-

ЗР– (ЗьР–) see, sight, view, light, vision, clear

ЗРАК– : зр-

ЗРЕЙ– ripe, mature

ЗУБ– tooth, *dent-*

ЗЫБ– vacillate, shake, shift, surge, swell

ЗЫВ– : зв-

ЗЯБ– sensitive to cold; connected with autumn plowing

ИГЛ– needle

ИГР– play

ИД– go

ИМ– have, possess, hold, take

ИМ(ЁН)– (← им-) name, *nomin-*

ИН– other

ИСК–[1] seek

ИСК–[2] : ист-

ИСКР– spark

ИСКРЕН– sincere, genuine

ИС-КУС– art, artificial

ИСТ– true, genuine

ЙД– : ид-

ЙМ– : им-

КАЗ–[1] show, indicate

КАЗ–[2] punish (← каз-[1])

КАЗН–[1] state, treasury

КАЗН–[2] (← каз-[2]) punish; execute

КАЙ– repent

КАК– how, *qual-*

КАЛ–[1] temper, harden; incandescent

КАЛ–[2] : кол-[2]

КАМ– stone

КАМЕН– : кам-

КАП– drop

КАР– punish

КАС– : кос-[3]

КАТ– roll, slope

КАЧ– roll, rock, swing, sway

КАШЛ– cough

КВАС– sour, ferment

КИВ– nod

КИД– throw, toss, hurl

КИН– : кид-

КИП– boil, seethe

43

КИС-	sour, *oxy-*; ferment	КОЛ-[3]	break, chop, crack
КИСЛ-	: кис	КОЛ-[4]	how much, *quanti-*
КЛАД-	place, put	КОЛД-	enchant, magic
КЛАН-	: клон	КОЛЕБ-	sway, waver, rock
КЛЁВ-	peck, nibble	КОЛЕС-	: кол-[1], wheel
КЛЕВЕТ-	slander	КОЛИК-	: кол-[4]
КЛЕЙ-	glue, stick, paste	КОЛОТ-	hammer, beat, knock, thrash
КЛИК-	shout, call	КОЛЬК-	: кол-[4]
КЛИН-[1]	: клн-	КОН-	end, final, limit
КЛИН-[2]	wedge	КОНЬ-	horse
КЛН-	curse, swear, oath; enchant	КОНЦ-	: кон-
		КОНЧ-	: кон-
КЛОН-	bow, incline, bend, lean, *-cline, -flect*	КОП-[1]	dig
		КОП-[2]	heap up, hoard, amass
КЛЮВ-	: клёв-	КОПТ-/КОПОТ-	smoke, soot
КЛЮЙ-	: клёв	КОР-[1]	submit, subject
КЛЮН-	: клюй-	КОР-[2]	reproach
КЛЮЧ-	key, *-clude, -clus-*, spring (water)	КОР-[3]/КОРН-	root, *radical*
КЛЯН-	: клн-	КОР-[4]	skin, rind, peel, crust
КНИГ-	book, *bibli-*, literary	КОРМ-	feed, nourish
КОВ-	forge	КОРОТ-	short
КОЖ-	skin, peel, *derm-*	КОС-[1]	cut, mow
КОЛ-[1]	round, ring	КОС-[2]	crooked, slanting, squinting
КОЛ-[2]	prick, stab		

КОС-[3] touch, *tang-*,
         -tig-, *-tact*

КОСТ- bone, *osteo-*

КРАД- steal

КРАЙ- (← крой-[1]) cut,
       border, edge; ex-
       treme

КРАП- sprinkle, spatter

КРАС- color, paint;
       beauty; red

КРАТ-[1] *ChSl* : корот-,
          brev-

КРАТ-[2] time (in a series),
          -fold

КРЕН- askew

КРЕП- strong, firm,
       fast, *fort-*

КРЕС- resurrect, revive

КРИВ- crooked, askance,
       curve

КРИК- shout

КРОВ-[1] blood

КРОВ-[2] (← крый) shelter,
          cover

КРОЙ-[1] cut (esp. cloth)

КРОЙ-[2] : крый-

КРОТ- mild, meek, gentle

КРОХ- crumble, crumb;
       small

КРУГ- round, circle, turn

КРУК- woe, grief, destruc-
       tion, failure

КРУП- large, huge

КРУТ-[1] steep, abrupt

КРУТ-[2] screw, twirl, turn

КРУХ- ruin, wreck

КРЫВ- : крый-

КРЫЙ- cover, close

КРЫЛ- (← крый-) wing

КУП-[1] bathe

КУП-[2] buy

КУП-[3] together, entirety

КУПОР- seal, plug

КУР-[1] smoke

КУР-[2] light, fair-haired

КУР-[3] fowl, chicken

КУС-[1] bite

КУС-[2] try, test, attempt

КУТ- wrap, wind

КУШ- : кус-[2]

ЛАГ- : лёг-[2], lay,
      -pose

ЛАД- smooth

ЛАЗ- : лез-[1]

ЛАЙ- bark

ЛАСК- affection, kind,
       caress

45

ЛГ-	(ЛЬГ-) lie, false	ЛИЦ-	: лик-
ЛЕВ-	left	ЛОВ-[1]	catch
ЛЁГ-[1]	light, easy	ЛОВ(К)-[2]	agile
ЛЁГ-[2]	lie, -*pose*	ЛОГ[1]	: лг-
ЛЁД-	: льд-	ЛОГ-[2]	: лёг-[2], put, lay, -*pose*, -*pone*
ЛЕЗ-[1]	climb, crawl	ЛОМ-	break, -*fract*-
ЛЕЗ-[2]	(← лёг-[1]) easy; useful	ЛОП-	break, burst
ЛЕК-	heal, cure, treat, *medic*-	ЛУК-[1]	bend, bow
ЛЕН-	lazy, sloth	ЛУК-[2]	separate
ЛЕП-[1]	fitting, proper; beauty	ЛУК-[3]	sly, cunning
ЛЕП-[2]	: льп-	ЛУП-	shell, hull, skin (verb)
ЛЕСТ-	: льст-, charm	ЛУЧ-	ray
ЛЁТ-	fly	ЛЫС-	bald
ЛЕТ-	summer, year	ЛЬГ-	: лёг-[1]
ЛИВ-	: лий	ЛЬД-	ice
ЛИЗ-	lick	ЛЬЗ-	: лез-[2]
ЛИЙ-	pour, flow, *flu*-	ЛЬЙ-	: лий-
ЛИК-	visage, face, person	ЛЬН-	: льп-
ЛИП-	: льп-	ЛЬП-	stick, adhere
ЛИСТ-	leaf; sheet (of paper)	ЛЬСТ-	flatter
ЛИХ-[1]	extra, superfluous; deprive	ЛЮБ-	love, like
		ЛЮД-	person, people, *popul*-
ЛИХ-[2]	bad, evil; wild, dashing, daring	ЛЮТ-	fierce, cruel, wild

МАЗ-	grease, smear, oil	МЕС-	mix
МАК-	(← мок-) dip, dunk	МЕСТ-[1]	place, local, *loc-*
МАЛ-	little, small	МЕСТ-[2]	: мьст-
МАН-	lure, entice, deceive	МЕТ-[1]	notice, note, mark
		МЕТ-[2]	aim
МАСЛ-	: маз-, oil, grease, butter	МЁТ-	sweep, hurl, throw
МАТ-	: мот-[1]	МЕХ-	mix; hinder
МАХ-	wave; miss	МЕЧТ-	dream
МГ-	(МьГ-) wink, blink	МЗД-	: мьзд-
МЕД-[1]	middle, mid-, *med-*	МИГ-	: мг-
МЕД-[2]	copper	МИЛ-	dear, nice
МЕДЛ-	slow	МИН-	pass, go by, skip
МЕЗД-	: мьзд-	МИР-[1]	peace, *pacif-;* world
МЁК-	hint, indicate		
МЕЛ-[1]	shallow, small, fine	МИР-[2]	: мр-
		МК-[1]	(МьК-) close, lock; adhere
МЕЛ-[2]	grind, mill		
МЕЛЬК-	flash, flit	МК-[2]	hurry, rush
МЕН-[1]	change, alter	МЛАД-	*ChSl* : молод-
МЕН-[2]	less	МЛЕК-	*ChSl* : молок-
МЕР-	measure	МН-[1]	(МьН-) think, *mem-*
МЁР-	: мр-	МН-[2]	(МьН-) crumple, rumple, knead
МЕРЗ-	vile, nasty		
МЁРЗ-	freeze	МНОГ-	many, *mult-, poly-*
МЕРК-	dim, dark	МОВ-	*ChSl* : мый-
МЁРТВ-	: мр-, dead	МОГ-	able (physically), might
		МОЙ-	: мый-

МОК–	wet	МУЖ–	man, husband
МОКР–	: мок–	МУК–[1]	torture, torment
МОЛ–[1]	pray, implore	МУК–[2]	flour
МОЛ–[2]	mill, grind	МУТ–	dull; confused, turbid
МОЛВ–	say, speak		
МОЛК–	silent	МЫВ–	: мый
МОЛОД–	young	МЫЙ–	wash, *lav-*
МОЛОК–	milk, *lact-*	МЫК–	: мк–[1]
МОЛОТ–	beat, hammer, thresh	МЫЛ–	soap, : мый–
		МЫСЛ–	thought, think
МОР–[1]	(← мр–) tire, exhaust; plague	МЬЗД–	reward, payment, retribution
МОР–[2]	sea, ocean, marine	МЬСТ–	(← мьзд) vengeance
МОРГ–	wink, blink	МЯГ–	soft
МОРОЗ–	frost, freeze	МЯК–	: мяг–
МОРОК–	: мрак–, dark, obscure	МЯС–	meat, flesh
		МЯТ–	disturb, confuse
МОРСК–	wrinkle		
МОСТ–	bridge, pave	НАГ–	bare
МОТ–[1]	wind, twist	НАГЛ–	: наг–, impudent
МОТ–[2]	squander, waste	НАДЕЙ–/НАДЁД–	hope (← ден–)
МОЧ–	← мог-т–		
МОЩ–	*ChSl* : моч–	НАДОБ–	(← доб–) necessary
МР–	(МЬР–) die, *mort-*	НАМЕР–	(← мер[1]) intend
МРАК–	*ChSl* gloom, dark	НАРОД–	(← род–) people, *popul-*
МСТ–	: мьст–	НАСЛЕД–	(← след–) inherit
МУДР–	wise	НАУК–	(← ук–) science, learning

НЕБ-/НЁБ-	heaven, sky
НЕБЕС-	: неб-
НЕГ-	tender, luxury
НЕДР-	internal, insides
НЕМ-	dumb (unable to speak)
НЁС-	carry (by hand), bear, -*pose*, -*fer*, -*late*, -*port*
НЗ-	(НьЗ-) penetrate, pierce, cut
НИЗ-[1]	down, low
НИЗ-[2]	string, thread; pierce (← нз-)
НИК-	penetrate, disappear, appear
НИМ-	: нм-
НИСК-	(← низ-[1]ск-) poor, poverty
НИЦ-	: ник-
НМ-	(НьМ-) take, grasp, *cap-*, -*cept* (see им-)
НОВ-	new, *nov-*, *neo-*
НОГ-	foot, *ped-*
НОЗ-	: нз-
НОЙ-	: ный-
НОРОВ-	: нрав-
НОС-	: нёс-

НОЧ-	night, nocturnal
НОЩ-	*ChSl* : ноч-
НРАВ-	*ChSl* disposition, temper; morals
НУД-[1]	want, need; force
НУД-[2]	bore
НУТР-	internal, inside (← утр-[2])
НЫЙ-	ache, hurt; whine, complain
НЫР-	dive, duck
НЮХ-	smell, sniff
НЯ-	: нм-

ОБЕД-	(← об-ед-) dine
ОБЁР-/ОБЁРТ-	: ← об-вёрт-
ОБЕТ-	*ChSl* promise (← об-вет-)
ОБИД-	offend (← об-вид-)
ОБИЛ-	abundant
ОБЛАД-	*ChSl* (← об-влад-) rule
ОБЛЁК-	(← об-влёк-) clothe, *vest*
ОБОРОТ-	(← об-ворот-) turn, *revol-*
ОБ-РАЗ-	form, image; educate
ОБРАТ-	*ChSl* ← об-врат- reverse, turn, *revol-*

49

ОБТ-/ОПТ- *ChSl* common, general, in quantity

ОБЩЕСТВ- social, society (← обт-)

ОБЫК- (← об-вык-) accustom, custom

ОБЯЗ- (← об-вяз-) obligate

ОГН- fire, *ign-*

ОДЁН-/ОДЕН- clothe (← ден-)

ОД(И)Н- one, single, lone, *uni-*

ОК- eye

О-ПАС- danger; apprehension, caution

ОПТ- : обт-

ОПЫТ- (← пыт-) experiment, experience

ОРУД- arm, equip, tool

ОСНОВ- base, foundation

ОСОБ- self, special, particular, person

ОСТР- sharp, acute

ОТ-ЛИК- distinguish

ОТ-НОС- relate

ОТЦ- (ОТЬЦ-) father, *patri-*

ОШИБ- mistake

ОЩР- : остр-

ПАД- fall

ПАК-[1] soil, dirty

ПАК-[2] pack

ПАЛ- burn, flame

ПАМЯТ- memory, : мн-[1]

ПАР- steam, vapor; soar

ПАС- tend, herd, pasture; store, supply

ПАХ-[1] smell

ПАХ-[2] plow

ПЕВ- : пей-

ПЕЙ- sing

ПЕК- care, concern

ПЁК- bake

ПЕН- foam

ПЕРВ- first, prime

ПЕРЁД- front, forward

ПЕРЁК- cross

ПЕСН- : пей

ПЁСТР- multi-colored, mixed

ПЕХ- foot

ПЕЧ-[1] : пёк-

ПЕЧ-[2] : пёк-

ПЕЧАЛ- sad, sorrow (← пек-)

ПЕЧАТ- print, seal

50

ПЕЩ-   *ChSl* : печ-[2]

ПИВ-   : пий-

ПИЙ-   drink

ПИЛ-   saw

ПИН-   : пн-

ПИР-[1,2] : пр-[1,2]

ПИР-[3] feast : пий-

ПИС-   write, draw, *scribe, script*

ПИСК-   squeal, squeak

ПИТ-   nourish, feed, *nutr-*; soak

ПИХ-   shove, push, cram

ПЛАВ-[1] swim, float, sail

ПЛАВ-[2] melt (caus. ← плыв-/плов-)

ПЛАК-   cry, weep, lament

ПЛАМ(ЁН)- flame : пал-

ПЛАТ-[1] pay

ПЛАТ-[2] cloth : плёт-

ПЛЁВ-   spit

ПЛЕМ(ЁН)- tribe, race, nation

ПЛЕН-   *ChSl* *capt-* : полон-

ПЛЕСК- clap, splash

ПЛЁТ-   weave, braid, twist, plait

ПЛОВ-   : плыв-

ПЛОД-   fruit, fruitful, fertile, bear

ПЛОСК- flat

ПЛОТ-[1] close, dense, firm, tight, compact

ПЛОТ-[2] flesh

ПЛОХ-   bad, poor

ПЛЫВ-   swim, float, sail

ПЛЮЙ-   : плёв-

ПЛЮСК- flat

ПЛЯС-   dance

ПН-   (ПЬН-) stretch

ПОВЕСТ- (← вед-) tell, tale, story

ПОДЛ-   base, low, mean

ПОДЛИН- real, genuine

ПОДОБ- like; seem, appear; be proper, fitting

ПОЗД-   late, tardy

ПОЗОР- shame (← зр-)

ПОЙ-[1] (caus. ← пий-) drench, water

ПОЙ-[2] : пей-

ПОКОЙ- peace

ПОЛ-[1] half; sex

ПОЛ-[2] floor

ПОЛЗ-   crawl, creep

51

ПОЛН- full, fill,
   -*plete, pleni-*

ПОЛОВ- : пол-[1]

ПОЛОН- *capt-*, capture

ПОЛОСК- rinse

ПОЛОТ- : плат-[2]

ПОЛЬЗ- use : льз-

ПОМН- remember : мн-[1]

ПОМОГ- help : мог-

ПОН- : пн-

ПОР-[1] rip, slash;
   thrash, flog

ПОР-[2] : пр-[2]

ПОРОЗ- empty

ПОРОК- (← рок-) defect

ПОРОХ- powder, dust

ПОРТ- spoil

ПОРХ- flit, flutter, fly

ПОТ- sweat

ПОШЛ- (← шьд-) trite,
   banal, hack

ПР-[1] (ПьР-) trample; go

ПР-[2] (ПьР-) shut,
   close; brace,
   support, press

ПР-[3] (ПьР-) argue,
   dispute

ПРАВ- right, *rect-*
   just, correct,
   ortho-; direct,
   rule

ПРАВД- = ПРАВ-ьД ← прав-

ПРАЗД- (*ChSl* for пороз-)
   empty, vain, idle,
   holiday

ПРАС- vain, idle

ПРАХ- *ChSl* : порох-

ПРЕД- *ChSl* : перёд-

ПРЕДЕЛ- boundary, limit
   : дел-[2]

ПРЕЗР- despise : зр-

ПРЁК- reproach

ПРЕС- fresh

ПРЕТ- forbid, prohibit

ПРИРОД- nature : род-

ПРИЯ- friendly, like,
   pleasant

ПРОБ- try, attempt,
   probe

ПРОДАЙ- sell : дай

ПРОК- firm, tight,
   secure

ПРО-МЫСЛ- industry
   (← мысл-)

ПРОС- ask, request,
   -*quire*

ПРОСТ- simple; pardon,
   forgive; take
   leave, part

ПРОТ-ИВ- against, oppo-
   site, oppose,
   anti-, contra-

ПРОШЛ–	(← шьд–) past	ПЬЯН–	drunk : пьй–
ПРУГ–	spring, resilient	ПЯТ–¹	spot, blotch
ПРЫГ–	jump, leap, spring, hop	ПЯТ–²	heel; back(ward)
ПРЫСК–	sprinkle; squirt -*ject*	РАБ–	*ChSl* work; slave
ПРЯГ–	harness, hitch; tense	РАБОТ–	*ChSl* : раб– work
ПРЯД–	spin (yarn)	РАВ–	(*ChSl* : ров–) equal, even, *equi*–
ПРЯМ–	straight, direct	РАД–	glad, joy
ПРЯТ–	hide, conceal	РАЗ–¹	strike, -*press*, -*flect*
ПТ–	fly	РАЗ–²	*ChSl* different, various, separate
ПУГ–	fright, scare		
ПУК–	bulge	РАЗ-ВИЙ–	(unwind =) develop
ПУСК–	: пуст–	РАН–¹	wound
ПУСТ–	let loose, re-lease, allow, -*mit*; empty	РАН–²	early
		РАСЛ–	: рост–
ПУТ–¹	confuse, mix, tangle	РАСТ–	: рост–
ПУТ–²	way, path, road	РАС-ТВОР–	dissolve, sol-vent; твор–
ПУХ–	swell, puff	РВ–	(РЪВ–) tear, rip, -*rupt*, break
ПЫЛ–¹	dust		
ПЫЛ–²	flame, fire, heat, passion	РД–	red, rust
		РЁВ–	howl, roar
ПЫТ–	try, attempt, prove	РЕВ(Н)–	jealousy; zeal, fervor
ПЫХ–¹	flare, puff		
ПЫХ–²	luxury	РЕД–	rare
ПЬЙ–	: пий–	РЕЗ–	cut, slice, carve -*grave*, -*cise*

53

РЕЙ- hover, swarm

РЁК-/РЕК- speak, say, name

РЁТ-/РЕТ- find, come upon, meet

РЕЧ- : рёк-/рек-

РЕШ- solve

РЖ- : рд-

РИС- draw, sketch

РИЦ- : рёк-

РОБ- meek, timid

РОВ- even, equal, smooth

РОД- bear, birth, *gen-, gener-, nat-*

РОЗ- separate (: раз-[2])

РОЙ-[1] : рый

РОЙ-[2] swarm

РОК- : рёк-

РОН- drop

РОПТ-/РОПОТ- murmur, grumble

РОС-[1] : рост

РОС-[2] dew, water, moisture

РОСЛ- : рост-

РОСТ- grow

РУБ- cut, hack, chop, hew

РУГ- swear, curse, scold

РУД- red; ore

РУЖ- outside, exterior

РУК- hand, arm, *manu-*

РУМ- red, ruddy

РУХ- crash, destruction

РЫВ-[1] : рв-

РЫВ-[2] : рый-

РЫГ- belch, *-ruct*

РЫД- sob

РЫЙ- dig

РЯД- order, row, rank

САД- (caus. ← сед-[1]) set, seat, *sed-*, plant

САМ- self, *auto-*

СВЕЖ- fresh

СВЕРК- sparkle, flash

СВЕТ- light, *lumin-;* world

СВИСТ- whistle

СВОБ-ОД- free, *liber-*

СВОЙ- own

СВЯТ- holy, sacred

СЕВ- : сей-

СЕД-[1] sit, seat, set, settle

СЕД-[2] grey

СЕЙ- sow

СЕК- chop, hack, cut, -*sect*

СЁЛ- (← сед-[1]) settle

СЕМ(ЕН)- seed

СЕМЬЙ- family

СЕР- grey, sulphur

СЕРД-[1] heat, anger

СЕРД-[2] : серед- heart, *cardi*-

СЕРЕБР- silver

СЕРЕД- middle, center, *med*-; heart

СЕСТР- sister

СИД- : сед-[1]

СИЙ- shine, radiate

СИЛ- strength, power

СКАЗ- (← каз-[1]) say, tell, speak

СКАК- : скок-

СКОБЛ- scrape

СКОК- spring, leap, jump, hop, gallop

СКОЛЬЗ- slip, slide, glide

СКОЛЬК- : кол-[4]

СКОР- quick, soon

СКОРБ- grief, woe, sorrow, offense

СКОТ- cattle, livestock

СКРЁБ- scrape

СКРИП- squeak, scrape, squeal

СКУК- bore

СЛ- (СЪЛ-) send

СЛАБ- weak

СЛАВ- glory

СЛАД- *ChSl* sweet (: солод-)

СЛЕД- trace, track, follow, heir, *sequ-*, *secu-*

СЛЕП- blind

СЛОВ- word, *log-*

СЛОВЕС- : слов-

СЛОГ- complex, compound (← лог-[2])

СЛОЙ- layer

СЛОН- lean, -*cline*

СЛУГ- serve

СЛУХ- listen; hear, *audi-*; rumor

СЛУЧ- happen, event

СЛЫВ- pass for, be known as

СЛЫХ- hear

СМЕЙ-[1] dare

СМЕЙ-² laugh

СМЕЛ- (← смей-¹) daring, bold

СМЕХ- (← смей-²) laughter

СМОТР- look, watch, observe, view, -*vision*, -*vise*, -*vey*

СН- (СЪН- ← СЪП-) dream, sleep

СОБ- special, particular, own

СОВ- push, shove

СОВЕСТ- conscience (← вед-)

СОЗД- : зд-

СОК- juice, liquid, soak

СОЛ-¹ : сл-

СОЛ-² salt, *sal-*

СОЛН-Ц- sun, *sol-*

СОЛОД- malt

СОМН- doubt, second thought (← мн-¹)

СОР- litter, trash

СОС- suck

СОСЕД- neighbor : сед-¹

СОХ- : сух-

СОЮЗ- *ChSl* union : уз-²

СП- (СЪП-) sleep

СПАС- save, rescue (← пас-)

СПЕЙ-¹ be on time, succeed

СПЕЙ-² ripe

СПЕЛ- : спей¹²

СПЕХ- : спей-¹ hurry

СПОР- (← пр-³) quarrel

СПОСОБ- means, device, way; capable

СРАМ- *ChSl* shame

СРЕБР- *ChSl* : серебр-

СРЕД- *ChSl* mid, mean, middle, *medi-* : серед-

СРОК- (← рок-) time limit, period of time

ССОР- quarrel

СТАВ- (caus. ← стой-) cause to stand, put, place, -*pose*

СТАН- become, begin to stand

СТАН-ОВ- put, stand; stop : стан-

СТАР-¹ old, ancient

СТАР-² try, attempt

СТАТ- : стан-

СТЁГ- button, close, fasten

СТЁКЛ- glass

СТЕЛ-	: стл-	СТРЕК-	excite, arouse
СТЕН-	wall	СТРЕЛ-	shoot; arrow
СТЕП-	step, stage, degree, *gradu-*	СТРЕМ-	strive, rush, aspire
СТЕРЁГ-	watch, guard	СТРИГ-	shear, clip, cut
СТИГ-	achieve, get, obtain, reach	СТРОГ-	strict, stern
СТИЛ-	: стл-	СТРОЙ-	order, (put into order =) build, *struct*
СТИР-	wash		
СТЛ-	(СТьЛ-) spread, cover	СТРОК-	line
СТОЙ-[1]	stand, *-sist*	СТРУЙ-	stream, current
СТОЙ-[2]	be worth, cost	СТУД-	freeze, cold
СТОЛ-	: стл- table	СТУК-	knock
СТОН-	groan, moan	СТУП-	step, stride, *-gress, -ceed, -cede, -cess;* act, deed
СТОР-	: стр-		
СТОРОГ-	: стерёг-	СТЫВ-	: стын-
СТОРОН-	(← стр-) side; country	СТЫД-	shame
СТР-	(СТьР-) stretch, expand	СТЫН-	grow cool, freeze, stiffen
СТРАГ-	*ChSl* : сторог-	СУД-[1]	judge, *judic-*
СТРАД-	suffer	СУД-[2]	vessel, ship
СТРАН-[1]	strange, foreign	СУЙ-	: сов-
СТРАН-[2]	*ChSl* : сторон-	СУН-	: суй-
СТРАН-[3]	(← стр-) expanse	СУТ-	*ChSl* being, existence, essence, nature, *-sent, -sence*
СТРАСТ-	(← страд-) passion		
		СУХ-	dry
СТРАХ-	fear, fright	СУЩ-	(← сут-) essential, essence

СЧАСТ– (← част–[1]) happy; luck, fortune

СЫЛ– : сл–

СЫН– son, *fili-*

СЫП–[1] pour, sprinkle, strew, scatter

СЫП–[2] : сп–

СЫР– damp, raw; cheese

СЫТ– satisfy, sate

СЫХ– : сох–

СЯГ– obtain, seize, grasp

СЯД– : сед–[1]

СЯЗ– : сяг–

ТАЙ–[1] hide, secret, *crypt-*

ТАЙ–[2] melt

ТАЛК– : толк–[2]

ТАСК– drag, pull

ТВАР– : твор–

ТВЁРД– hard, firm

ТВОР– make, do, create, *-fy*

ТЁК– flow, run

ТЕЛ– body, *corp-*

ТЕЛЕС– : тел–

ТЁМ– dark

ТЕН– shade, shadow

ТЁП– warm, heat

ТЕР– lose

ТЕРЗ– tear

ТЕРП– bear, endure, stand

ТЕС– (cf. тиск–) close, tight, narrow

ТЁС– hew, cut, scrape, finish

ТЕХ– comfort, amuse

ТИР– : тр–

ТИСК– press, squeeze; print

ТИХ– quiet, calm

ТК– (ТъК–) poke, weave

ТЛ– rot, decay, corrupt

ТОВАР– good(s), commodity, ware(s)

ТОК–[1] sharp, point; exact

ТОК–[2] : тёк– flow, current

ТОЛК–[1] sense

ТОЛК–[2] push, shove; pound

ТОЛОК– : толк–[2]

ТОЛСТ– fat

ТОМ–	weary, tire, oppress	ТРОН–	: трог–
ТОН–	thin, fine	ТРУД–	labor, work, difficulty, *labor*, *oper*–
ТОП–[1]	: тёп–		
ТОП–[2]	sink, drown	ТРУС–	coward
ТОПТ–/ТОПОТ–	trample, stamp	ТРЯС–	shake, tremble, cause to tremble
ТОРГ–[1]	trade	ТРЯХ–	: тряс–
ТОРГ–[2]	thrust; lift, elevate	ТСК–	vain, useless
		ТУГ–	tight; sad, grief
ТОРЖЕСТВ–	solemn; celebration, triumph	ТУК–	fertile, fat
ТОРК–	jut	ТУП–	dull, blunt
ТОРОП–	hurry, rush	ТУСК–	dull, dim
ТОСК–	yearn, weary, oppress	ТУХ–	extinguish; spoil
		ТЬМ–	: тём–
ТР–	(ТьР–) rub	ТЫК–	: тк–
ТРАВ–	herb, grass; poison	ТЯГ–	pull, tug, *-tract*, *-tend*; heavy weight
ТРАТ–	lose; spend, waste		
		ТЯЗ–	: тяг–
ТРЕБ–	demand, need, require; use, consume	ТЯН–	: тяг–
		ТЯП–	hit, chop, hack
ТРЕЗВ–	sober		
ТРЁП–	beat, strike, stamp; shake about, tear	УВ–	: уй–
		УГЛ–[1]	corner
ТРЕПЕТ–	tremble	УГЛ–[2]	coal, carbon
ТРЕСК–	crack, split	УД–	fish, angle
ТРОГ–	touch	УЗ–[1]	narrow

УЗ-[2]	bind, bond, fetter, tie	ХЛЕБ-[1]	gulp
УЗД-	bridle, rein, restrain	ХЛЕБ-[2]	grain; bread
		ХЛОП-	slam
УЗЛ-	knot : уз-[1]	ХЛОПОТ-	trouble, care; solicit
УЙ-	shoe		
УК-	accustom,(accustom to =) teach, learn	ХМЕЛ-	tipsy, intoxicate, hops
УЛ-	street, lane	ХМУР-	gloomy, cloudy; frown
УМ-	mind, intellect	ХОД-	go, come, pass, -gress, -cede, -ceed, -cess
УСЛОВ-	condition, convention : слов-		
УСПЕХ-	success : спей-[1]	ХОЗЯЙ-	boss, owner, landlord, host
УСТ-	mouth, oral	ХОЛ-	care, groom
УТР-[1]	morning	ХОЛОД-	cold
УТР-[2]	womb, inside	ХОРОБ-	brave, good
		ХОРОН-	bury
ХВАЛ-	praise	ХОРОШ-	(← хороб-) good
ХВАСТ-	brag, boast	ХОТ-	wish, want
ХВАТ-	grab, seize, catch; be sufficient	ХРАБ-	: хороб-
		ХРАН-	: хорон- -serve
ХВОР-	sick, ill	ХРИП-	hoarse
ХВОСТ-	tail	ХРОМ-	lame
ХИТ-	grab, seize	ХУД-	thin; bad, poor
ХИТР-	(← хит-) sly, crafty, cunning	ХУДОЖ-	art, handicraft
ХИЩ-	(ChSl ← хит-) predatory	ХУЛ-	censure; blaspheme
ХЛАД-	ChSl : холод-		

60

ЦАР-	tsar, emperor, king, royal, *reg-*	ЧЁТ-	: чт-[1,2]
ЦАРАП-	scratch	ЧИН-[1]	rank, order, *ord-*
ЦВЁТ-/ЦВЕТ-	color; flower, bloom, *flor-*	ЧИН-[2]	make, do, cause; fix
ЦЕД-	filter, strain	ЧИН-[3]	: чн-
ЦЕЛ-[1]	whole, entire; kiss	ЧИСЛ-	(← чт-[1]) number, *num-, numer-*
ЦЕЛ-[2]	goal, aim	ЧИСТ-	clean, pure
ЦЕН-	price, value	ЧИТ-	: чт-[1]
ЦЕП-	chain, catch, hook	ЧЛЕН-	member, limb
		ЧН-	begin
ЧАЙ-	expect, await, hope	ЧРЕД-	*ChSl* : черед- institute
ЧАР-	charm	ЧТ-[1]	count; consider; read
ЧАС-	hour, time, clock		
ЧАСТ-[1]	part, share	ЧТ-[2]	honor, esteem
ЧАСТ-[2]	often, frequent	ЧУВ-	: чуй-
ЧЕЗ-	(dis)appear	ЧУД-[1]	not one's own, strange, alien
ЧЕРЕД-	line, row, rank, turn, alternate	ЧУД-[2]	marvel, wonder
ЧЁРК-	sketch, line, draw	ЧУДЕС-	: чуд-[2]
ЧЁРН-	black	ЧУЙ-	feel, sense, *-path-*
ЧЕРП-	draw up, draw out, scoop	ЧУТ-	: чуй-
ЧЁРСТВ-	stale		
ЧЕРТ-	line, feature, draw	ШАГ-	step, stride
ЧЁРТ-	devil	ШАЛ-	prank, mischievous
ЧЁС-	scratch, comb	ШАТ-	shake, stagger
ЧЕСТ-	(← чт-[2]) honor	ШВ-	: ший-

ШВЫР-   hurl, throw

ШЁД-   (ШьД-) : ход-

ШЁПТ-/ШЁПОТ- whisper

ШЕСТВ- : шёд-

ШИБ-   shove, push, hit

ШИВ-   : ший-

ШИЙ-   sew

ШИР-   wide, broad

ШУМ-   noise

ШУТ-   joke

ШЬД-   : ход-

ШЬЙ-   : ший-

ЮЗ-   *ChSl* : уз-[2]

ЮН-   *ChSl* young

ЮТ-   shelter, refuge

Я-   : им-/ьм- take

ЯВ-   appear, obvious, real, show, display

ЯД-   eat; poison, *toxi-*

ЯР-   bright; harsh, fierce, raging

ЯСН-   (ЯС-ьН-) clear, plain, bright

ЩАД-   spare, mercy

ЩЕДР-   generous

ЩЁЛК-   click, snap

ЩЕМ-   squeeze, pinch

ЩЕП-   chip, split

ЩИП-   pinch, pluck

ЩИТ-   shield, (de-)*fend*

ЩУП-   feel, grope

ЩУТ-   perceive, *percept-*

ЬМ-   : им-

SOME OTHER BOOKS FROM SLAVICA

Howard I. Aronson: *Georgian: A Reading Grammar,* 526 p., 1982.

James E. Augerot and Florin D. Popescu: *Modern Romanian,* xiv + 330 p., 1983.

Natalya Baranskaya: Неделя как неделя *Just Another Week,* edited by L. Paperno *et al.,* 92 p., 1989.

Adele Marie Barker: *The Mother Syndrome in the Russian Folk Imagination,* 180 p., 1986.

Karen L. Black, ed.: *A Biobibliographical Handbook of Bulgarian Authors,* 347 p., 1982.

Marianna Bogojavlensky: *Russian Review Grammar,* xviii + 450 p., 1982.

Rodica C. Boţoman, Donald E. Corbin, E. Garrison Walters: *Îmi Place Limba Română/A Romanian Reader,* 199 p., 1982.

Richard D. Brecht and James S. Levine, eds: *Case in Slavic,* 467 p., 1986.

Gary L. Browning: *Workbook to Russian Root List,* 85 p., 1985.

R. L. Busch: *Humor in the Major Novels of Dostoevsky,* 168 p., 1987.

Gary Cox: *Tyrant and Victim in Dostoevsky,* 119 p., 1984.

Michael S. Flier and Richard D. Brecht, eds.: *Issues in Russian Morphosyntax,* 208 p., 1985.

Charles E. Gribble, ed.: *Medieval Slavic Texts, Vol. 1, Old and Middle Russian Texts,* 320 p., 1973.

Charles E. Gribble: *Reading Bulgarian Through Russian,* 182 p., 1987.

Charles E. Gribble: *Russian Root List with a Sketch of Word Formation, Second Edition,* 62 p., 1982.

Charles E. Gribble: *A Short Dictionary of 18th-Century Russian/*Словарик Русского Языка 18-го Века, 103 p., 1976.

Morris Halle, ed.: *Roman Jakobson: What He Taught Us,* 94 p., 1983.

William S. Hamilton: *Introduction to Russian Phonology and Word Structure,* 187 p., 1980.

Michael Heim: *Contemporary Czech,* 271 p., 1982.

Michael Heim, Zlata Meyerstein, and Dean Worth: *Readings in Czech,* 147 p., 1985.

Warren H. Held, Jr., William R. Schmalstieg, and Janet E. Gertz: *Beginning Hittite,* ix + 218 p., 1988.

M. Hubenova & others: *A Course in Modern Bulgarian, Part 1,* viii + 303 p., 1983; *Part 2,* ix + 303 p., 1983.

Richard L. Leed and Slava Paperno: *5000 Russian Words With All Their Inflected Forms: A Russian-English Dictionary,* xiv + 322 p., 1987.

Edgar H. Lehrman: *A Handbook to Eighty-Six of Chekhov's Stories in Russian,* 327 p., 1985.

Maurice I. Levin: *Russian Declension and Conjugation:* A Structural Description with Exercises, x + 159 p., 1978.

SOME OTHER BOOKS FROM SLAVICA

Alexander Lipson: *A Russian Course. Part 1,* ix + 338 p., 1981; *Part 2,* 343 p., 1981; *Part 3,* iv + 105 p., 1981; *Teacher's Manual* by Stephen J. Molinsky (who also assisted in the writing of Parts 1 and 2), 222 p.

Sophia Lubensky & Donald K. Jarvis, eds.: *Teaching, Learning, Acquiring Russian,* viii + 415 p., 1984.

Horace G. Lunt: *Fundamentals of Russian,* xiv + 402 p., reprint, 1982.

Paul Macura: *Russian-English Botanical Dictionary,* 678 p., 1982.

Vasa D. Mihailovich and Mateja Matejic: *A Comprehensive Bibliography of Yugoslav Literature in English, 1593-1980,* xii + 586 p., 1984.

Edward Mozejko, ed.: *Vasiliy Pavlovich Aksenov: A Writer in Quest of Himself,* 272 p., 1986.

Alexander D. Nakhimovsky and Richard L. Leed: *Advanced Russian, Second Edition, Revised,* vii + 262 p., 1987.

Temira Pachmuss: *Russian Literature in the Baltic between the World Wars,* 448 p., 1988.

Lora Paperno: *Getting Around Town in Russian: Situational Dialogs,* English translation and photographs by Richard D. Sylvester, 123 p.

Slava Paperno, Alexander D. Nakhimovsky, Alice S. Nakhimovsky, and Richard L. Leed: *Intermediate Russian: The Twelve Chairs,* 326 p.

Jan L. Perkowski: *The Darkling A Treatise on Slavic Vampirism,* 169 p.

William R. Schmalstieg: *Introduction to Old Church Slavic, second edition,* 314 p., 1983.

Peter Seyffert: *Soviet Literary Structuralism: Background Debate Issues,* 378 p., 1985.

J. Thomas Shaw: *Pushkin A Concordance to the Poetry,* 2 volumes, 1310 pages total, 1985.

Oscar E. Swan: *First Year Polish, second edition, revised and expanded,* 354 p., 1983.

Oscar E. Swan: *Intermediate Polish,* 370 p., 1986.

Charles E. Townsend: *Continuing With Russian,* xxi + 426 p., 1981.

Charles E. Townsend: *Czech Through Russian,* viii + 263 p., 1981.

Charles E. Townsend: *Russian Word Formation, corrected reprint,* viii + 272 p., 1975.

Boryana Velcheva: *Proto-Slavic and Old Bulgarian Sound Changes,* Translation of the original by Ernest A. Scatton, 187 p., 1988.

Susan Wobst: *Russian Readings and Grammatical Terminology,* 88 p.

Что я видел *What I Saw* by Boris Zhitkov, Annotated and Edited by Richard L. Leed and Lora Paperno, 128 p. (8.5 x 11" format), 1988.

For a complete catalog (currently containing about 140 titles), write to Slavica Publishers, PO Box 14388, Columbus, Ohio 43214 or call 614-268-4002.